Over the Hill

with a

Magic Carpet

Dedications

I dedicate this book to the memory of my beloved husband **Jack** – John Emerson Skinner – who was mostly responsible for, and guided us through, the many journeys recorded on these pages

to **Paul Daniels**
for his enthusiasm and support

to **Ken Dodd**
in whose rib-tickling shows we were delighted to appear

and to Professor **Eddy Dawes**
who welcomed us into the world of Magicians

Over the Hill
with a Magic Carpet

from the diaries of

Joy Skinner
of
'Emerson & Jayne'

Fern House

First published in 1999 by
Fern House
High Street   Haddenham
Cambridgeshire CB6 3XA

www.fernhouse.com

A catalogue record for this book
is available from The British Library

ISBN 0 9524897 5 9

Jacket by Chris Winch Design

Printed in England by TJ International Ltd, Padstow

Emerson & Jayne and the Magic Carpet
(not forgetting Sammy Snake)

Acknowledgements

I would like to thank Rodney Dale for his perseverance
in organising a mass of material and making it into a book

Zoë Dale and Matt Pettitt for fitting the text and illustrations together

Tom Dolezal for teaching me to use the computer

and last, but not least, the retired dancers Burke and Kovak, returned
from managing shows in Paris, Beirut and Las Vegas, who have helped
run the 'Barnstormer's Retreat' during the creation of this epic.

Introduction
by Paul Daniels

I am a professional magician. Day in, day out, every week, month and year, I read magic books and magazines, devouring the knowledge of new and ancient magic. Conjuring, really. The secrets of those performers, myself included, who pretend to have magicial powers. I love my business. I love all theatre. To children I describe the theatre as a space-ship of the imagination. 'Once you sit down inside it you can go anywhere, to the outermost reaches of fantasy.'

Of course that rarely happens. You have fun, cry, are moved in differing ways, but there are certain moments when the performance will take you, almost against your will, and make you forget where you are, who you are, and what you know cannot be.

In my club, stage and television career I have seen – literally – hundreds of acts, but when I am asked which were the most magical moments I can name but a few from the world of theatre in general and two from the world of magic in particular. This book is about the working life of the creators of one of those Wonder Full moments. Yes, the spelling is deliberate.

I had heard about the act of Emerson & Jayne. I had been told that their carpet flew. I knew that it was described as a 'black-light act', which uses the peculiar nature of ultraviolet light on certain treated materials and makes them glow. Emerson & Jayne were in pantomime in Sunderland and I was working in the local clubs. The opportunity was not to be missed so, full of knowledge, off I went and bought a ticket.

Perhaps I caught it on a bad day but the pantomime was too verbose. Too much script and not enough action. The kids (include me in there) were bored. Even the star comedian had lost his voice and was whispering the responses to our shouts. I cannot even tell you which pantomime it was.

The first half was coming to an end when on came two dancers in beautiful Oriental costumes which, it seemed to me, owed a lot to traditional Balinese design. The 'pro' in me immediately knew that these costumes had not come from the stock wardrobe – they were too good. The Oriental dancing was obviously not the work of the show's choreographer either. It was far better. This was a good, quality act, *from the moment when the performers entered and before we had seen them work!*

I noted that Emerson & Jayne – for that is who they were – had beautifully toned bodies. Both were in great condition and this was emphasised in their movements and agility. Somewhere in the back of my mind the magician in me noted that they were performing in full stage lighting. They were against black curtains and their costumes did seem to be bright but I was unaware of black light being used.

Their dance style was perfect, fitting the music and costumes, and suddenly the audience – for the first time that evening – sat entranced.

It was a long time ago now, but I remember a particular movement they made with two tall parasols, wrapping their legs around the poles. With quite a small movement of the leg the upper ends of the parasols would move in a wide arc, both of them absolutely together. Emerson carried the parasols off amid great applause.

My memory of what happened next may not be totally accurate; I did not take notes and the act did go through minor changes both before and after this performance. It will, I hope, still give you a feeling of sitting beside me on that evening.

As Emerson left, Jayne pulled on an Eastern-style basket. In other shows I understand that a couple of candles were brought on and other small props but on this occasion I only remember her dragging on the basket and producing a small trumpet-like musical instrument. I also remember that she looked the epitome of every young man's dream of a harem girl – petite, slim, beautiful.

As she started to play the instrument a bird flew on, flew around, perched on the end for an instant, peered into the trumpet, pulled out a brightly coloured worm and flew off with it. Jayne got over this interruption and started to play again. Another worm came out of the end of the trumpet and wiggled its way into the basket.

A bright pink flamingo came on and indicated that Jayne's music was upside down. The snake written on the music was upside-down. (Snake on the music? Don't even think about it. By now we were in another world.)

The music was corrected, Jayne played and a snake started to rise out of the Oriental basket – and rise, and rise. It was huge and chased her around the stage until she drove it off with a broom. The basket, music stand and other bits went off at the same time.

Then Jayne spotted a smallish carpet centre stage and went to sweep it with the broom. The carpet rolled itself up. As Jayne flattened the rolled up end the other end rolled up behind her. When she stood in the middle of the carpet both ends rolled up. This simple clown action was very, very funny – and made so by the comic body language of the performer. Jayne, both in the basket routine and the carpet routine, proved herself to be a great visual comic without losing any of her charm and femininity.

Eventually she threatened to beat the carpet with the broom and – Wonder of Wonders – the carpet FLEW. It took off and hovered several feet above the stage. Jayne tried to push it down to the floor again but the carpet was not having it. Is it my memory or did she *really* run behind it to push it down from the back? That's what I remember and it drives the magician in me crazy.

She left the carpet hovering, went to the front of the stage and picked up a short, very short, length of rope and indicated in mime that it was obviously not long enough. What would you do if you really *could* do magic? She stretched it until it was very, very long, and coiled it on to the stage. She picked up the trumpet and, as she played, the rope rose into the air. This was better than the Indian Rope Trick; this rope formed a ladder-like stairway with a 'hook' at the top which hung on nothing.

The carpet was then pushed to the stairway sideways through the air. Would she? Could she? She did. Jayne climbed the rope 'ladder' and sat on the carpet. She pulled the rope which instantly fell to the floor. AND THEN SHE FLEW.

The Magic Carpet carried her up, down, from side to side, twisted in the air and then out, out, out over the orchestra pit and over the audience. Jayne the Wonderful Genie or Slave of the Ring or whatever was smiling down at us and waving as she flew from one side of the theatre to the other, back on to the stage and into the wings. There WAS Magic in the World and how the audience roared their approval! My hands were sore as Emerson & Jayne took their bows.

It was afterwards that I realised even more how wonderful it had been. I, the great know it all, the professional magician with the mountains of knowledge, had not only enjoyed great magic, I had enjoyed Great Theatre. I had not noticed the transition into full black light. I had had all my knowledge and beliefs suspended by a Master and Mistress of Theatrical Craft.

The years go by and the act of Emerson & Jayne has been copied by people who think that if they own the equipment they can do the act. They cannot. The reason is usually that they are inelegant magicians. They do not have the style, the strength, the beauty, the design, the music, the elegance, the comedic body language, the total package that made the act work. They have a piece of equipment, but they will never have the Magic that was Emerson & Jayne and the Flying Carpet.

Have I raved on too much? I can't. I loved the moment so much. When I was offered a proof copy of this book to read I realised that here was a way to say 'Thank You' for the experience and for the memory, which has never faded. Then I read the book, made up of memories regenerated by diaries, and I realised that it's as close as you will get to feeling what Show Business for the working professional is really like.

Oh, yes. By the way, despite her self-deprecation in the book, Joy is still beautiful.

Publisher's introduction

In 1940 the government instructed my Father, who was unfit for military service and hoping to do a PhD in Anglo-Saxon at King's College, to become a porter at Addenbrooke's Hospital in Cambridge. Jack Skinner, a conscientious objector, had also been drafted there. It was not long before each recognised the other's qualities, and they entered into partnership making handbags (mainly for the nursing staff at the hospital) in our attic at 142 Chesterton Road, Cambridge.

Jack had a fascinating array of tools and patterns, materials and accessories, and I spent many happy hours in the leatherwork shop giving expression to my own talents by making a catalogue of handbag designs and rigging up various devices to make the work easier.

At the same time (as this book will tell) Jack and his wife-to-be Joy were dancing with the Ballets Jooss and I saw them perform at the Cambridge Arts Theatre; the most memorable pieces (to a boy of nine) were that legendary ballet *Green Table*, and a scene in *Seven Heroes* where Milkmaid Joy put her bucket over Jack's head and led him off stage.

Jack was probably the first adult I got to know, apart from family and schoolteachers (who necessarily had a certain aloofness), and he gave me a new view of what people could be like; he was quiet and kind, had a wonderful sense of humour and immense creativity. He was one of the formative influences on my life and we never lost touch.

When I was stationed near Folkestone during my National Service, Jack's flat at Lee Green was a favourite stopping place, about half way home to Cambridge. And it was there that I first heard of the birth of 'Emerson & Jayne' and saw some of the props Jack was making for the emerging Act. As the years passed, Jack and Joy moved to Barnstormers and worked on the barn, and we stayed there from time to time (though they were more often than not away in some far-flung place of entertainment). Sometimes they visited us and, as the Act reached the height of its development, we went to see the Magic Carpet flying in places such as Blackpool, Norwich and Scarborough.

In 1993, Emerson & Jayne at last decided to retire after an amazingly long and energetic career. We went to their farewell run at the Players Theatre, Charing Cross – a wonderful performance, and a meeting of crowds of fans from over the years. Sadly, Jack had too little time to enjoy his retirement, and to work on the memoirs; fortunately Joy has completed the work and I am privileged to have been asked to produce this book celebrating a wonderful couple and their unique contribution to the world of entertainment.

Rodney Dale

A Note on the Title
by Jack Skinner

The man in the office of the *pension* explained that the £200 was a deposit we should pay in case we damaged the furniture and another £2 in case we lost the key. I paid up and said I didn't think it was likely we'd do much damage, showing him the tears in the linen he'd already given us in case he charged us for them and he agreed. He obviously didn't like foreigners, let alone 'ARTISTES'! He then said: 'I don't expect you'll do a lot of damage – after all, you are over the hill'. This little man with a chip on his shoulder and a manner cross between school teacher and prison warder was quite right and without knowing it had given us the title of our proposed memoir – *Over The Hill with a Magic Carpet*.

It could be a good time to start writing in this apartment on Balfour Street in Haifa as we are here for a month at least. Why do I want to write a book? Perhaps because I have not chosen to reproduce some part of myself in the normal way as a member of this species and yet would like to leave some trace of being alive in the twentieth century . . .

Joy Skinner continues

. . . And now it is twenty years and more later and sadly Jack died before he could start the book. We were to write alternate chapters and now it is left to me to write them all. As I enjoy writing, why not? The life we shared in those days of trains, hotels, cars and theatres was so wonderful, it's worth writing about! Being so much older now 'over the hill', as the Israeli said, is a most appropriate phrase, and I feel like adding to the title – 'and far away'. However it must be 'with a Magic Carpet' as it was in the later years when we became a Speciality Act doing the Halls, Pantomime and Cabaret.

My husband never kept the many diaries I did away back to the thirties, so I know the early reminiscences will sound rather one sided. First I will try to relay what he told me of his childhood . . .

John Emerson Skinner

Jack, as he was always called, was a strapping ten-pound baby born to a diminutive mother who required sixteen stitches after his exit in a Lewisham nursing home on 15 January 1915.

Many years later he wrote in his diary: 'the self-centred, withdrawn person that I am now is not far removed from the child I became in the years 1915 to 1925. It was not that I was an unwanted child but the years did not allow me to have a normal childhood. I was packed off to a wet nurse for some weeks which, I believe, was not unusual in those days. I was collected when my parents moved to Manchester, where I spent the first few years of my life. Not long after, my parents were sent to prison for being pacifists. In prison, my father contracted tuberculosis in the joints of two limbs; luckily my mother was released and was able to take him nourishing food. She put me to bed in the afternoon with a tray of plasticine hoping I would amuse myself in her absence. But I was too small to be left alone and what sad little grey animals I made in those long afternoons! As the light failed, I knew some awful fate had befallen my Mother.'

Jack's father was a journalist, a kind, gentle and intelligent man. His wife was older than him; it was her second marriage. We guessed she had been sexually incompatible with her first husband – when we furnished our first flat she was determined that we should buy separate beds. She had disliked Jack's first girlfriend, labelling her 'A mess of Pottage'! She was charitable and kind nevertheless, was very small and ran everywhere, turning up at the most unexpected moments. I was terrified of her.

Allen Skinner, Jack's father

Jack's mother would help with the wardrobe at the theatrical school run by Margaret Morris and J D Ferguson, and one felt she would have liked to have had a theatrical career herself – which obviously resulted in her encouraging Jack, who had no craving to become a dancer but was sent at an early age to Margaret's school where he learnt composition, stagecraft and costume design, as well as how to teach and direct.

The MM children were given a school education by visiting teachers.

An early performance for Jack at Margaret Morris School

They also took elocution lessons with a tall eccentric lady called Madame D'Estelle who, Jack told me, wore a long woollen garment with no underwear beneath it. (We wondered how the children knew this.) In 1927

Jack at Margaret Morris school

Jack joined the cast of *Peter Pan* at the Palladium with Jean Forbes Robertson as Peter. Jack was 'Nibs' and toured several times with the show. He recounted how rough the wolves were in the pillow-fighting scene with the lost boys – Matron (who looked after them off stage) had to read the riot act many a time.

He also toured in *Topaz*, a play with Raymond Massey in the lead, where there was a scene with school children. When older, Jack gained useful theatre experience in the Little Theatre with Nancy Price. He stayed with Margaret Morris, directing and

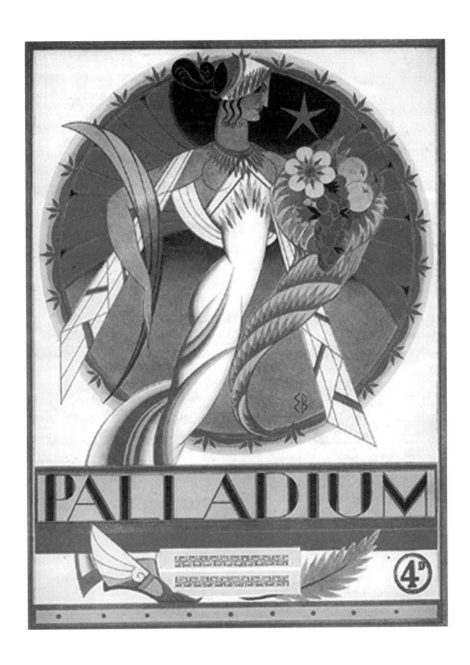

Peter Pan, *1927*

composing, until he visited a performance of the Ballets Jooss at the Gaiety Theatre. He decided that this was definitely for him and before I left Dartington for the Summer break, I noticed Jack's name on the list of Summer School pupils.

Joy Bolton-Carter

I was the third in the family of four Bolton-Carter children and, in contrast to my husband, had a happy early childhood in the company of my younger brother John. We played in a high-fenced garden behind a large Victorian house opposite Leicester's Victoria Park. My father was a surgeon at the Leicester Infirmary and married a nurse from that establishment. Patients would often visit him in the afternoons and, as his consulting room looked out on to the garden, we were constantly in trouble for noisy behaviour. We slept up in the gabled night nursery with Nanny, drifting off to the rumble of tramcars passing up London Road, their upper deck lights sending the pattern of our leaded windows circling the room.

We girls – Vivien, Joan and I – and a few other little friends had lessons with a Miss Pywell who taught us the piano. Brother John must have started his schooling when we were all old enough to attend day schools, and my elder sisters went to share a governess with wealthy friends on their farm outside Leicester until we were all sent off to boarding school.

Joy, Ma, Pa and Joan

We looked forward to the glorious family holidays we spent at Blakeney in Norfolk, either messing about in boats or wading across the muddy marsh to the National Trust Bird Sanctuary on the Point.

As for my interest in the Dance, that all started in Miss Flecknoe's babies' class in the church hall room where mothers and nurses sat round the walls while we children danced the polka. It's amazing how a gratifying result fans the ego – they applauded me!

I shall never forget the pleasure of receiving my first pair of little pink toe shoes from Italy when I was about eight years' old – opening them secretly on the bend of our winding stairs and smelling the fragrant satin with ecstasy.

Joy (top, third from right) at St Felix school

When I was 13, I joined Joan, my second sister, at St Felix, the boarding school at Southwold in Suffolk, where it was possible to take athletics and the Dance and to excel in hockey, cricket and lacrosse teams, and even to take extra dancing classes provided by an excellent and attractive Bedford College teacher – on whom I soon had a crush. I enjoyed the art classes immensely. One girl painted the most marvellous pictures and I learnt that this Gwynneth Johnston was a daughter of the artist Augustus John. I loved school; most of the teachers were good and we got an excellent education in every subject. Famous artistes often came and gave concerts in the big hall, and John Galsworthy had written our school song.

Sister Joan left for Oxford and I remained at school another year receiving a grounding in German – though I did not know that I would study in that country for the next three years, and certainly never dreamt that it would be another six years before I would meet Jack, the man who would become my husband.

Having launched myself into the idea of a career in Dance, I found that I had begun to grow apart from my family, and increasingly distant from the lifestyles and interests of my siblings, though I did my best to relate to them whenever possible.

Germany

Sister Joan was learning German from two ladies who taught Oxford undergraduates in their vacations near Jügenheim in the Bergstraße. Mother decided that we should visit her on holiday, planning to leave me there as I had by then finished at St Felix. We stayed in this idyllic countryside for a while, finding out which was the best dance school in the country, and decided that they considered the Jooss Leeder School, which had its studios at the Volkswang Schule in Essen, would be the

Joy (left) at the Pension

answer. However, we then learnt that Jooss had been invited by the Elmhursts to migrate to Dartington Hall, near Totnes in Devon. The Elmshursts knew far better than we did what soon was to happen to art in Nazi Germany.

Next to Jooss, the Mary Wigman School in Dresden was the favourite, so off we all set on the first part of a long journey in an old-fashioned open car through woods and wonderful new country, dropping the two Frauen off at some friends of theirs. We stayed the night in the Schwarzwald; then continued on by train to Dresden.

I well remember ringing the bell of an imposing mansion set in a large garden overlooking the Elbe. The basement and lower floor were occupied by Frau Gutbier, an art dealer's wife, and her four sons; we had been told that this lady took in students from the Wigman Schule which was a little lower down the Bautznerstraße.

Frau Gutbier opened the door on to a hallway where hung four large Homburg hats. Mama almost started back down the steps at the thought of leaving her 17-year-old daughter in what looked like a rather posh brothel.

However, here it was that I stayed during my time in Dresden under the care of this fearsome-looking Frau. I discovered later that there was a Herr Gutbier who occasionally visited but guessed that the little man had found a less overpowering mate after producing the sons!

I found that Frau Gutbier adored the Führer and would queue for hours to 'Heil Hitler' him should he visit the town. As for the sons, I never saw them don those Homburg hats, as they usually were obliged to wear the brown caps of their Nazi contingents. Only the eldest son appeared to be serious about Hitler, and wore the smart black uniform of a storm trooper. He sometimes arrived on a powerful motorcycle. I was once treated to a ride on its pillion.

Herbert, the second son, rather plump and nicknamed Pumpy, played the piano and was the most artistic. Ebi, the third son, was unattractive and seemed to know it, always keeping in the background. When I was not at school I spent a lot of time with the youngest son Viechel (German for 'Little Beast'), a mischievous fellow of 14.

After settling me in a nice large room with a small balcony overlooking the Elbe, next door to a friendly German girl called Elly, a secretary working in the town, Mama and I went down to the Wigman Schule – a nice modern building with three studios, office, and changing room with communal wash pool – a popular gathering spot for gossip. There seemed to be no male students; I soon learned that Mary's theatre group was all female, with her as the central figure.

We were then introduced to Elisabeth Wigman, Mary's sister, who auditioned me in my little Greek tunic, dancing around the large studio as I'd learnt to at school. I was accepted in spite of Mother's eager suggestions that my feet were far too flat for a dance career. 'On the contrary,' Elisabeth retorted, 'it will cure them.' There were several American students in the school, some living in Frau Gutbier's *pension* who could help me when my school German was insufficient.

Mary was no Nazi but there was among the teachers one who definitely was, and the government had instructed him to include Rassenkunde – the study of race – in the curriculum. We attended his classes with tongue in cheek and, though we disliked him, he gave quite good lessons in technique.

The Modern Dance stemmed originally from Isadora Duncan, who started the break from the Classical style, both in America and Europe. In America, Ruth St Denis started her version of the Dance, influencing Martha Graham who later opened her school in New York. In Europe, the technique became known as Central European. Mary Wigman was an ex-pupil and friend of Rudolph von Laban, and therefore taught his technique and notation. Laban often came to watch the classes; later he was to flee to Jooss in England.

My limited dance classes in England had taught my body that it must strive to attain perfection, and so the hard slog began.

We were required to compose dances to show at the end of each term, and we gained experience of performing before an audience at functions around Dresden – indeed, I remember dancing 'April' in a floral cape round the Zwinger Pillars, later bombed by the RAF.

When I think back to those days I realise how immature I was but I soon found out how kind and helpful my teachers and fellow pupils were to one so green. Even Frau Gutbier, behind that masterly bulk, kept a watchful eye on everyday happenings. In those days, there being no TV, we would attend French and German classes, go to *Thé Dansants* in Dresden, meet music students in other parts of the town, listen to Marlene 'Falling in love again' on the wireless and, on showing our student card, were admitted almost free to the opera house.

In the holidays, when not travelling home to England, I would go skiing in the Riesengebirge with the Gutbiers. I still have a dear little carved insect-like figure holding a forget-me-not as a staff, much repaired by Jack, in my bedroom. She's nearly as old as I am, the little dear! She's come all the way from the snows of the Erzgebirge.

Mary had an international reputation in the modern dance world sending out performers and teachers to other countries – hence the large number of foreign students in the school. I was told of Louise Salberg and Leslie Burroughs, who had not so long since finished their training and returned to England. Both were highly spoken of and it was suggested that I should contact them when I returned home.

Mary had travelled in the East and being in stature no Lilac Fairy or Giselle was influenced by dancers of those countries. She taught us to move every part of our bodies rather than to concentrate on disciplined leg technique, and hired a classical dancer to teach us this. Our hips, torsos, arms *etc* learned to lead us into intricate curves and circles, and we became masters of turning for hours, whirling like Dervishes!

My schoolfriend Irmgard and I were always hungry as a result of all these endeavours, and my diaries seem to record every meal I ate. My vegetarian diet must have got burnt up very quickly with such unwonted exercise! Very conveniently, on our way home up the Bautznerstraße was a baker who sold the most delicious Käse Kuchens.

Joy at the Wigman Schule

My first efforts for the end of term – sometimes public shows – were a lullaby to a Brahms serenade and a grimacing pirate. Needless to say, probably owing to my protruding front teeth, the pirate was the success.

That Christmas I went skiing with the Gutbier family in Silesia. I had done a year's training at the school already. Mary Wigman had no permanent group at the time and was doing solo performances here and there. I saw her on stage for the first time in Dresden Albert Theater and was most

Dresden Theater

impressed – as was our whole school, judging by the almost hysterical applause we gave her. It sounded like a pop group's audience of today. Mary's *Dance of the Earth* and *Death Dance* were very fine, though I imagine the critics of today might consider them too emotional. Mary was always talking of the 'Seele' and the 'Gestalt' in our theory classes. However, she danced a delightfully spirited gypsy number to follow. Some time later Laban visited the school in order to choose dancers for a show he was putting on in Berlin. He used members of Mary's original group with the addition of students he considered suitable, and I was one of the lucky ones!

Mary took most of the rehearsals in preparation for this show as it featured some of her dances along with some very good solos by members of the group and a dance by my teacher Gisela.

So from now on, in addition to daily classes, we rehearsed every evening and learnt something about a famous artiste's temperament. Mary had very little patience and would scream at anyone who made a mistake. But she could be so sweet and gentle when everything went well, and was exceedingly magnanimous later when the shows were a great success in a neighbouring town and she invited us all to a meal to celebrate.

In the summer break Mama, with sister Joan, and a Leicester friend and her son, decided to pay me a visit. Thinking back, I'm sure it was Mama's last hope of drawing me back to a conventionally safe life by the possibility of marrying the son, though we had often met at parties and had never been attracted to one another.

The night of their arrival all the trains were late. Whispers rumoured that something sinister was afoot and indeed it was what we now call the Night of the Long Knives.

Only then did we realise how frightening the National Socialists were. Getting into the tram outside our school with an American Jewish fellow student one day, I heard people whispering quite audibly 'JUDEN', at which everyone turned and stared at us.

My diaries of the thirties are written in German; the ink is faded and difficult to decipher. It's strange how little I remember of those days, but the diaries do make me realise what a wonderful dance training Mary gave us. Her dedication was often mocked as 'very German' by some folk, but at that time I would never have benefited as much from a dance education at home.

Before the summer holidays the students of my year took their examinations in all subjects relating to the dance. I must have passed satisfactorily as I was awarded a certificate that says I may teach dancers in the Wigman method. I never took up that occupation as I was summoned to Mary's presence to be told that I could join her touring group – as long as I remained a student in status, receiving only my travel fares and eight Marks a day to live on. What Glory! My poor little friend Irmgard from Leipzig was heartbroken to be excluded in favour of a foreigner. I must say it was strange for Mary to be allowed to engage me when the Socialists were becoming more Nationalist from day to day. As a student, however, they were not employing me.

I was to meet Mama and Joan on the Island of Rugen for a holiday, catching up with an American fellow student and her mother later. This

An early performance for Joy (bottom left) at the Wigman Schule

turned out to be a traumatic fiasco, as I waited at the railway station for them throughout the day and night, becoming more anxious and more lonely as the hours passed. At about midnight I was relieved to be approached by a friendly-looking soldier who must have noticed my distress. On learning of my predicament he volunteered to help me find a hotel somewhere near. It never occurred to me that he might not have had honourable intentions as he left me at the door. Today I would be a lot wiser – but then I am more knowledgeable of what can happen to damsels in distress. I will never forget the memory of my first encounter with an enormously comforting German quilt that night in the Station Hotel; it was heavier than any of the duvets we use these days, and completely engulfed me.

There was a telegram the next morning telling me that Joan was ill with her period and could not travel. They never did make the journey, but I have a picture of me and my friend Letitia playing our recorders happily on a yacht at sea.

Wigman Tour 1935

I had hardly been anywhere in England, and yet before I was twenty I had travelled the length and breadth of a foreign country, and performed in over a hundred towns including Amsterdam, the Hague, Stockholm and Malmö. I can't remember whether Danzig was then Polish or German, but we traversed the Polish Corridor to it.

It was on my twentieth birthday that I nearly missed the train at Dresden Hauptbahnhof for the start of the trip to Sweden where Drusilla and Gisela were waiting anxiously with a bunch of birthday flowers for me.

Mary, well known from her previous tours, received invitations for us to meet members of the royal family, and we were surprised to see how freely they moved among their citizens in the streets at that time without (as far as I could judge) bodyguards. And they shook hands with us all. Earlier, on our arrival, officials had greeted us, asking which of us was a Fräulein Carter. Not being famous, I was astounded to be presented with yet another bunch of flowers. They had seen from my passport that it was my birthday !

I was the youngest of our group, and considered rather vulnerable, but I seldom felt nervous of the new surroundings. I must confess to secretly hoping I would be allotted a double room in the hotel with Ilse, a mature and knowledgeable girl who later married Karl Klasen, who became President of the Deutsche Bank. She would kindly take me on a tour of every town to discover its fine ancient churches and treasures and introduce me to old master paintings in the many richly filled art galleries.

Mary Wigman on the boat to Sweden, 1935

In later times when performing in Hamburg's Hansa-Theater, we were always welcome at their home outside the town.

On arrival in a town we would be given the name of the hotel and of the room companion we would share with. Hotels varied vastly in each town – from humble to grand – as did the theatre conditions. Sometimes we were in a hall without curtains or adequate dressing rooms; sometimes in a single room. As we were partly doing a '*Kraft Durch Freude*' (Strength Through Joy) tour – Hitler's idea of pleasing the masses – we had to entertain in small humble cities as well as large attractive ones. The Nationalist Socialists must have been footing the bill.

I still can picture some of the dancers: they were all German, except for Drusilla, an American, and myself. There was Muck (a nickname – really Dorothea) a niece of the renowned sculptor and architect Mies Van Der Rohe, a friend of Gisela's called Erica, and Fee. All of us had to unpack, train and rehearse in the theatre after we had settled in to the hotel; otherwise the day was ours to explore our surroundings and rest. It was a tiring life as we had often travelled a long distance from the

The Wigman Tour, 1935 – Joy in front on the left

previous town and we were frequently invited to parties after the show.

At the end of one of those journeys, I was struggling from the train with a rather heavy bag, when it pulled me out and across the great buffers. Luckily, I wasn't squashed between them with that metallic clashing sound, but what a shock it was – my colleagues rescued me and I recovered with a brandy in the station canteen. Soon it was back to Dresden to pack for Berlin, the Olympic Games and then home.

In Berlin, our group was greatly enlarged by dancers from the Wigman school. We rehearsed on the grass of the enormous arena; I think we danced to Beethoven in a great circle, Mary in our midst following Kreutzberg, a famous German dancer of those times. I suppose at the time we felt honoured to be appearing at the games before Hitler and his cronies, as Leni Riefenstahl made his film of the 1936 Olympics. At the time, we did not realise how influenced Leni was by Hitler and his regime; he was such a fine artiste!

Mary had an international reputation in the modern dance world sending out performers and teachers to other countries – hence the large number of foreign students in the school. I was told of Louise Salberg and Leslie Burroughs, who had not so long since finished their training and returned to England. Both were highly spoken of and it was suggested that I should contact them when I returned home, for at the end of the week it was off to Hamburg to catch the Bremen for England. Little did we know that England and Germany would soon be at war.

Autumn holiday

I had been instructed on arrival home to contact an ex-Wigman dancer often warmly spoken of during my time in Dresden and now teaching in London. This was the aforesaid Lesley Burroughs, wife of Leon Goossens, the oboe player. She advised me to study further with Kurt Jooss, now settled at Dartington Hall in Devon.

Kurt Jooss

The Ballets Jooss had recently won a Grand Prix in Paris for him with the famous *Green Table*.

Could I persuade my parents to pay further school bills for my dance career? Especially as a doctor friend's wife and ex-teacher had heard of the progressive co-ed school at Dartington where the children were allowed to use the swimming pool unclothed. She did not know that this modern school was at least a mile from the dance school, and that the two were in no way connected.

In spite of this, my wish was generously granted and, after the usual Norfolk holiday, Mama, Joan and I set off for Devon.

The Green Table *(Gentlemen in Black)*

Dartington Hall

It turned out that, as a result of Jooss's triumph in Paris with *Green Table*, the autumn term was flooded with new students of many nationalities. In consequence, the dancers' sleeping quarters were all occupied by the time I arrived at the Hall, and I had to be billeted down at the village with the

dance school's caretaker, sharing a room with Monica Johnston who has remained a friend to this day. How cold it was later in November and how glad we were to move up to the dancers' flats in the courtyard. Our landlady had talked a great deal; I wrote in my diary what she told us of her first husband – how he had had one buttock blown off during the war which caused him later to throw himself out of the window to his death!

The students were of all shapes and sizes, mostly female. The first day of term

Joy at Dartington Hall

all solitary-looking newcomers were auditioned together in the larger studio, and placed in one of three classes; to start with I was to join the middle class.

Jooss had been a pupil of Laban, who had influenced the Wigman Schule; being a devotee of his, Lisa Uhlmann was to take our class. We had to learn about such things as Choreutics and Eukinetics which, if I remember correctly, were to do with movement in space and movement in quality or expression. But I found that Jooss's technique needed more strength than Wigman's, especially in the legs, and I envied those who had had a training more classical than mine.

Lisa Ullmann's and Sigurd Leeder's classes saw to that, and I worked very hard through 1937 and 1938 until Jooss formed what was then called the Studio Group with Toschka the rather excitable Pole, Birgit Cullberg who was later the leader of Swedish Ballet, another Swede called Barbro, my friend Monica Johnston,

Sigurd Leeder

and me. I think we all hoped to be soon incorporated into the Ballets Jooss; meanwhile, we were supposed to work for ourselves, but to attend the school technical classes, composing solo and group compositions.

We no longer lived in the dancers' quarters but moved down to our own rooms in the staff part of the junior school. We ate up in the Hall's large dining room.

Dartington Hall

By the end of that year Hitler was looming nearer and nearer and our Jewish artistes must have been growing very nervous. One of the teachers, Miss Bock, was leaving and Jooss asked me if I would like to teach in the school from the following term. In retrospect, I wonder if he thought that, should there be a war, his school might remain intact, if peopled only by non-Germans. In the end Jooss took Monica and myself in to the ballet much to our delight, as well as Toschka the Pole who had been in the company before. Toschka's husband was in the Polish Diplomatic service and during our tour we heard he'd been found in his American hotel bedroom asphyxiated by being smothered with a pillow. Alas Jooss, Leeder and others were to be interned on the Isle of Wight when war broke out, and the dance school was used for army billets but, before this catastrophe, a tour of England and America was scheduled for which we started rehearsing in the new school studio, joining our friend Bunty Slack, already a year in the Company.

Dartington was indeed a Utopian Community as Michael Young described it in his book *The Elmhursts of Dartington*. I knew nothing of its evolution until I read the book; I knew only of the Children's School (with the mixed nude bathing) and the Dance School (where I was). How lucky I was to spend almost three years in the place where we dancers were not the only ones to be given haven.

I learned that Leonard Elmhurst, after leaving Cambridge, instead of entering the church as his clergyman father had expected, went to study for a degree in agriculture in America. He had wondered 'if it were necessary to be a Christian in order to become a Christian'. This extremely Christ-like man, who was not rich, met the widowed and rich Dorothy Straight in New York and again at Cornell University. After a long friendship, and after Leonard had visited India, influenced by and learning from Rabindranath Tagore, Dorothy agreed to finance the purchase of an estate in England on which to build a Utopia.

Leonard and Dorothy married and Leonard found the ideal spot among the 14th-century Dartington buildings above Totnes in Devon. Dorothy followed later with her three children; together they set out to create this educational Utopia.

When I arrived, apart from the Children's School down the hill, there were some old buildings that had been renovated and turned into studios and living space with a small theatre at the entrance of the courtyard, all surrounded by a farm. It was a very large community which housed not only the Jooss family and his dancers, but painters, musicians, actors and many different craftsmen. Michael Chekov ran the theatre school, Hein Heckrot and Mark Toby gave art classes, and Willy Soukop sculpted. Sometimes famous artistes would come to entertain in the theatre; sometimes we would gather for gramophone concerts up in the cosy room

Sailing at Blakeney

in the tower. There was no television, of course, so we would often go down to the cinema in Paignton or Torquay with boy friends, mine usually a pianist. We would also visit the moors for picnics or the Devon coves in summer for a swim. It was all very innocent. We travelled in a small Ford car my father had given me on my twenty-first birthday. Sigmund Freud and Bertie Russell sent their children to Dartington school where the youngsters were far less liberated than was rumoured.

There was only a short summer vacation for the students who had been enlisted into the Group. I went to Blakeney and sailed with Viv in Restless and Whirlwind, winning a spoon as trophy at Wells. We bathed and sunned on the Point, sometimes sleeping in the hut which was then quite well equipped. The National Trust resented private owners of huts there in the sand hills but could not claim the ground they were built on until they crumbled with the years or their owners did.

We then visited Cambridge, where my brother was newly ensconced in his rooms at Trinity. We punted on the river, but kept hitting the banks as he had not yet achieved the knack of wielding the punt-pole.

It was soon time to return to Dartington to start rehearsing. Mama was very depressed at my departure; she had obviously hoped that my ideas of a dance career would wear off and that I would find a nice Leicester husband! To make matters worse, my Dartington boyfriend Laurie, whom I really loved through his music and gentle nature, arrived to accompany me back to Dartington. She need not have worried; he was shortly to take up a teaching job at Christ's Hospital School.

We all thought Chamberlain had persuaded Hitler to leave us alone for the time being so Jooss went ahead with his new ballet – *Chronica Sinistra*. This was obviously politically motivated as there was a fierce dictator in it governing a country like Italy in the middle ages. There were many scenes in it but it never received the acclaim that *Green Table* did. A little man called Bouchène designed elaborate and costly costumes for it, for which Dorothy Elmhurst undoubtedly paid. Of the first scene, I remember that we all held hands in a circle, and that the German dancer Ervin I was attached to was robed in pea-green tights.

The Summer School had just finished and group rehearsals were in full swing for the next tour. They were held in the new studio overlooking an orchard full of trees loaded with the most delicious apples which we often stole on the way to the Barn Theatre to try out a finished scene on the little stage.

We new ones were to learn the rest of the repertoire which was most exciting, especially as three of us were to understudy the Young Girl in

Green Table. Noelle de Mosa, the present Young Girl, was most diligent and helpful – as were all the members of the Ballet for all the roles we had to learn in the other works. The easiest ballet to learn was Ravel's *Pavane* in which we were all stern Spanish courtiers whose deliberately wooden movements seemed to crush the poor little Infanta. Swedish Eva Leckstrom could have walked out of that picture of the Infanta in the museum, so closely did she resemble her with her reddish locks.

We had also parts in *Seven Heroes, Big City* and other ballets to learn. Kurt Jooss spent his time, often rather slowly, with couples, solos *etc* for *Chronica*. His mind was still occupied with the thoughts and effects of a probable war on his work and his family. He was constantly called away from the studios to attend emergency meetings to discuss plans for evacuating refugees before Chamberlain's return from Europe.

If there was spare time and free space, we still occupied ourselves with our own creations. Mine were a Smetana polka, Schumann's *Scenes from Childhood, Despondency* to a Rachmaninoff Prelude, *Jackanapes* and *Stillness* to a Brahms lullaby . . . I remember the titles but little else apart from the utter spiritual satisfaction I got from performing the Rachmaninoff and the glow in my heart when my efforts received praise from Kurt Jooss!

In November 1938 we were to do a children's charity show up in London at the Cambridge theatre, my first performance with the company. We were to do only two ballets: *Ball in Old Vienna* and *Big City* where I was to do my duet with the young man in *Bal Musette*. The Vic Wells, London Ballet, a modern company and various soloists were also taking part.

We travelled by bus from Dartington, staying the night in London as rehearsals were to be on stage early the next day. I remember Jean Beddels on her points accompanied by a piano in the wings as we waited our turn, though I recall nothing else beyond suffering from a bad state of nerves during our rehearsal. Bunty Slack's mother came in the afternoon and pronounced our part of the show the most entertaining, so I needn't have worried.

I got home to Leicester for a short family Christmas with friends. Joan was home from South Africa having broken up from her Oxford boyfriend, and Viv was recovering from the sad loss of a brand new husband, after a fall from his horse, causing a tumour on the brain. John, three years my junior, also arrived from Cambridge. Mama, so kind, pretty and loving to us all, made me feel guilty all the time as I knew she was so against my leaving and yet the home environment was becoming more and more alien to me.

DARTINGTON HALL PRESENTS
(SEVENTH SEASON 1938-9)

DIRECTOR: KURT JOOSS

RETURN VISIT TO

THE OLD VIC

MAY-JUNE, 1939

PROGRAMME

The Old Vic, 1938

Later in life I wrote the following ditty, entitled:

A Mother's Lament

Our dear Mama has many cares beside Bazaars and such affairs, the
cause of which are four offspring, perhaps unlike most human beings.
They've all desired to leave the nest to satisfy some strange bequest.
That fluttering urge within the breast!
The eldest, she is very brave, she has a horse and rides to hound
jumping the highest fences round,
And yet her life is not one dream of happy youth as it may seem
to horsey friends in Leicester fields.
Joan is Mama's biggest care, forgetting oft to do her hair
and somehow, when in social haste, even forgets about her face.
Such children with a useful brain and good appearance should refrain
from making themselves look rather plain.
The third, she is a dancer fair, may this soon Mama learn to bear.

But all the same, it breaks her heart, that no rich man rose from the Dart.
The youngest is no big problem and actually there's naught to blame.
He calmly took what was beget, following in Father's step.
And so he should, with some ambition, tread the future with decision
At Cambridge to become physician.
But every family has its trials, its fits and starts and little wiles
And little birds will leave the nest, seeking life's hard experience.

Ballets Jooss – First Tour

Arriving back at Dartington, summer 1938, to start rehearsing once again,
I noticed a list of Summer School students on the notice board. One of
these names was Jack Skinner. I knew a Jack Skinner of the shoe people,
Lilley & Skinner; we had sailed in the same boat at Blakeney. It seemed
strange to me that that Jack would take a summer dance course – he
wasn't the type! However, I thought no more of it until two of the male
dancers had to be replaced, and Jooss recruited this Jack as one of them.
He was certainly not Lilley's Skinner, though this fellow didn't much
resemble a dancer either – more an athlete wearing shorts instead of
dancer's tights.

At that time there were no female vacancies in the troupe; the German
nationals were still praying, like us, that Hitler wouldn't dare to invade
this sceptered Isle. Nevertheless, Jack's girl friend Audrey Seed, principal
dancer of Margaret Morris, had followed him hopefully to Dartington,
then attending the autumn school term. Not till the end of the war did

Audrey join the company, staying in the School when it moved eventually to Cambridge. Her husband then was the pianist John Cook who later became the ballet accompanist. But this was later; now we would stare at this handsome couple as we fed between rehearsals in the White Hart.

Later, in the final rehearsals for *Chronica*, I found myself grasping the hand of the pea-green tights again. It was Jack Skinner. I thought nothing of it, being betrothed to my pianist boyfriend Laurie who was to come down to Dartington soon to give a recital. The former wearer of the green tights, a German, had left England with his friend – we heard later they had been spies, but we never found out if this was true.

The Chekovs gave a party in the Big Hall for which we dancers all climbed into respectable clothes rather unwillingly as we knew the VIPs would all be there. Apparently Michael Young was to move that School to America; they gave a farewell performance in the theatre. Mrs Elmhurst played the part of Aase in *Peer Gynt*. Another pleasant evening was Mrs Christy's guest concert in the theatre.

As it was not yet time for our tour to begin, we were able to move into the big house in Totnes where the Chekovs had stayed. Luckily I still had the little Ford so that I could bring Bunty and Monica up to the studios each day and we used Martin Penny's loft room above the studios when not rehearsing. Jooss had now finished *Chronica* and had begun his new ballet *Spring Tale*. In this, Monica and I were Leaf Maidens in the wood scene and Jack Skinner a Wood Witch in the most realistic tree costume, all of which were designed by Heckrot. Ulla Soederbaum was the most delightful Princess in the court scene and Bunty Slack a gorgeous Mistress of Ceremonies.

After Christmas, rehearsals began for the tour which was to start at the end of January when I was at last to travel through the towns of my own country, having already visited most of Germany's. The first town on the list was Stratford-upon-Avon followed by Cambridge, Leicester, Oxford, Sheffield, Newcastle, Manchester, Glasgow, Edinburgh, Cardiff, Bournemouth, Eastbourne and Brighton. Somewhere in the midst of this tour we took part in a Dartington-sponsored performance of Handel's opera *Rodelinde* at the Old Vic, also doing a week of Ballets Jooss.

It was scorching hot in June; Monica and I had a room in Covent Garden almost over the market halls and were awoken at the crack of dawn each day by the crashing of crates and boxes all around us. Sleepily we would wend our way to the theatre over the Hungerford Bridge to work. After the première of *Rodelinde*, *The Times* wrote a kind criticism praising the courage of the Dartington Arts Department in dealing with

Jooss as Death in Green Table

Handel: 'Great singers were needed for his operas and these voices were not strong enough'. The *Daily Telegraph*, however, gave praise to Stan and Roddy, the male leads.

We stayed long enough in London to meet friends and relations and somehow found the time away from the theatre to visit museums, Hampstead, Kew Gardens and other sights for the first time – and even attended a matinée of Ruth Draper's one-woman show, sitting enthralled for over two hours as she vividly portrayed a succession of characters on a stage bare of scenery or props.

Leicester, after ghastly digs in Cambridge alleviated by my brother's companionship and the use of his rooms in Trinity, was most exciting for me but also daunting, for I had to prove to a critical family that I wasn't a failure, and had also to shine in the eyes of their friends so as not to let them down. Jooss had allowed me to take over the part of the Young Girl that week in *Green Table* in which, together with other parts, I think I was able to make quite a good impression. It was easy to dance well, as the Opera House was full every night with a noisy and enthusiastic audience.

Jooss did not accompany us throughout the whole tour, his family – Aino and the children – having remained at the house in Dartington. Aino was an Estonian and had often directed the rehearsals; with war almost upon us and, being perhaps of Jewish blood, the family was very occupied with future plans. When Jooss was with us he always danced the part of Death in *Green Table*; otherwise it was a fine strong German fellow called Rudolph Pescht. At the time we had in the company several Germans, Swedes, Swiss, Dutch, Lithuanian, Hungarian and four English: Bunty, Monica, Jack and me. Rudy was a very fine figure of Death in the skeleton costume, with superb ghostly spot lighting, but I enjoyed Jooss's interpretation somewhat more. This was his stern fierce expression of final fatality which would turn then to a comforting finality with each victim of war. I experienced this at my death in scenes when dancing the Old Mother or the Young Girl, and it is something I have never forgotten.

By August (1939), back at Dartington, there was commotion. Foreigners were warned by the Home Office to pack their bags and anti-Nazis told to burn any pictures of Hitler *etc* as there were sure to be spies around! Read *Mein Kampf* and you were a spy immediately. I wrote in my diary: 'Please God, don't let there be a war'. Everyone around the estate was looking worried. Chamberlain had set off once again to see Hitler who was now busy slaughtering the occupants of Danzig and would soon be in Poland. Holland was mobilising.

So as not be on the wrong side of the channel in the event of war, four patriotic members of the company left for Germany: our stage manager and his wife and our very good *Green Table* Profiteer and his wife Emma. New dancers and a stage manager had to be enlisted. Bert our barman came along as stage manager, as well as David Grey, a Dutchman called Lucas Hoving, and a Latvian named Lydia Kyascht.

A week later we were at war, making blackout curtains and expecting our contracts to be terminated. Part of the dance school was to be given over to the Land Army, though a nucleus was to remain. To us younger dancers it seemed the end of everything – especially the foreign tours that had been scheduled.

Jooss summoned us all and explained that we were still under contract and that the autumn tour would go ahead. Holland naturally was cancelled, but the American tour still held good, war permitting. Fritz Cohen, our musical director, would be in charge as Jooss was not to accompany us – indeed, he and Sigurd Leeder were to be interned on the Isle of Wight for a short time. Later mother and her friends in their Leicester Red Cross war effort canteen were horrified that Jooss should send dancers through the perils of the Atlantic after the Germans had just torpedoed the *Athenia*, tipping two American dancer friends of mine into the ocean after attending Jooss's Summer School. They had both been colleagues of mine in the Wigman Schule; I heard later they had been rescued.

Naturally *Green Table*, an anti-war subject, could not be included in the British repertoire; *Chronica*, a fitting topical replacement was therefore to be rehearsed, with a restaging of the *Prodigal Son* in new costumes.

The Elmhursts returned from a visit to the USA, having met and talked at length with Roosevelt who had hopes that Dartington could continue with its high standards in teaching a moral and Utopian way of living. He spoke then of what the Common Market was supposed to be achieving fifty years later!

In October we left for Bristol, followed by Stratford, Norwich, Blackpool, Manchester, Aberdeen, Glasgow, Edinburgh, Bedford, Ireland and Cambridge before a return to Dartington to pack our bags for the trip to America. Little did we know that, as a group, we would never return to our Utopia at this lovely place.

It was a relief when the Statue of Liberty and the skyscrapers of New York appeared out of the mist – though maybe our friend Bunty was a little sad, having fallen in love with the Dutch ship's doctor en route.

After lengthy immigration and customs formalities, we were transported by our Impresario Greanin and the Columbia Concerts representative to our comfortable hotel with private bathrooms; what a luxury after those landlady's digs in Manchester!

That evening we discovered that the famous Martha Graham was giving a recital in the town which, of course, the Company was keen to attend, and did so with delight.

In January 1940 we started on a tour through sixty towns; my diary finishes on 4 April with a rather childish poem:

> I have seen more dawns and sunsets than most on misty hills
> And passed by so much beauty one stared in disbelief
> And ever left it standing, a stranger in this world.
> Is nature with this beauty no stimulant to man?
> Another path to follow? Another course to run?
> Perhaps he does not notice or seek beyond his shell
> For what might raise him higher above this Wartime Hell.

We moved on from day to day and had very little time to explore the many towns, each one looking so like the others; it was a question of unpacking, rehearsing, performing, packing, and sleeping again, often on the train. It was a very severe winter, and how glad we were to reach California and its palm trees.

We all caught bad colds or flu at the beginning of the tour. Fritz Waldmann – known as 'Twin' – was the second pianist; he became very ill and had to be left behind in a Baltimore hospital. It was very difficult for Fritz Cohen alone to play the music of *Chronica*; it was hard enough to dance to. Finally he had to engage a deputy – indeed at one time we had three pianists around. But for the time being, we had to perform the alternative programme which consisted of *Seven Heroes, Big City, Ball in Old Vienna* – and *Green Table*, which we could present as America was not yet at war. Sometimes I was given Jack Skinner as a partner which was very agreeable! He and I took many frozen walks around Philadelphia but were able to thaw ourselves in the fine well-heated museum there.

We performed in many universities and high schools which was a new experience as the young audiences were so enthusiastic. Stepping out of the train in Richmond we were confronted by banks of snow, no transport and closed shops. Our secretary was told that it was the heaviest fall of snow they had had in forty years; there could not possibly be a performance that night, the town having no snow-clearing equipment.

If it had not been for a tiring walk after a very long journey we dancers would have welcomed the news of a free evening but, after waiting for orders in a large hall of the city while talk of broken contract guarantees went on, our hopes of that treat faded. We had to trudge all the way back to the station in order to move on to our following date. It was quite usual on the tour to cover enormous distances, sometimes made easier at night by the most amazing metamorphosis of our railway carriage. As darkness approached, the steward would appear and change the whole area into curtained rows of bunks on each side of the centre walkway. The bunks were most comfortable and we woke up to a completely different scene; this time it was one of orange groves and palm trees in tropical warmth. We were heading south towards Jacksonville, the Gulf of Mexico, and over to Cuba.

Havana was very beautiful with its Spanish buildings. Jack had a Margaret Morris friend staying in the opulent part of the town who acted as our guide; it was before Castro, and we saw many beggars. I would have liked to have had a swim in the inviting sea but the friend told us the sharks sometimes swam quite close to the shore.

We visited the oriental gardens where romantic music wafted through bushes, and stone ballerinas posed in arabesques by storks and little orange trees. On the way out, like naughty children, we couldn't resist turning all the little signposts in different directions to confuse the visitors.

When we left, Jack bought a large sack of oranges from one of the small boys who were selling them on the platform. Always resourceful, he sold the individual oranges to us, making himself quite a profit, and leaving quite a few oranges in his own bag too!

The Gentlemen in Black on a hot day in Miami (Joy is second from the left)

On President Roosevelt's birthday, we left the flag-bedecked streets of Tampa by bus to catch a train for Miami. Here we were to learn how strong the unions were in America, as the stagehands would not allow anyone but themselves to handle props or furniture used on stage. This was fatal for the green table, accustomed to being carried on stage in a split second in a blackout by we politicians about to gesticulate each side of it. In another town, we had already experienced a union strike where they had managed to bar us from the hotel that had been booked for us.

So many different towns – it is hard to remember them or their theatres but special experiences still remain in the memory such as passing through the Rocky mountains, visiting Niagara Falls and marvelling at the white cloud of spray over the Horseshoe Falls. Then there was the sky at night crossing over to Cuba; I have never seen such a magnificent firmament of bright stars.

By the end of March Columbia Concerts had sent us to theatres, high schools and auditoriums from the Statue of Liberty in the east to the Golden Gate Bridge in the west; through snow and blizzards to tropical warmth, and back again to winter. Sometimes we remained in a place only one day, the theatre our hotel, and the train sleeper our bed. Often we had to meet town bigwigs after a show and hold polite conversation over a dainty cheese pasty before packing and hurrying off to the station. It was no wonder we could not describe every town we visited. What luxury it was when we stayed a few days in one place with a comfortable hotel, good art gallery and large theatre. Battle Creek – the home of Kellogg's Cornflakes – was one of these with an impressive auditorium like a coliseum. Its ceiling was painted blue and, when lit up, seemed to be open to the sky.

These were the days when Disney was turning out his first feature-length films and we had time to go and see the latest – *Pinocchio* – which didn't then appear as childishly cute as it does to us now - after all, we were young. I was twenty four the day after Easter and Jack was already twenty five. It was easy with all this travel and novelty to forget about war and the people at home.

When we arrived in Canada, though, the atmosphere changed, bringing us back to reality. Males were joining up and drilling to go overseas. The Germans were torpedoing more of our ships and becoming a greater menace each day. My brother's American friend from Cambridge, whose family I had stayed with in New York, went to join the RAF as a navigator, only to be shot down and killed on his first flight over Germany. Letters arrived from home about the family's war work. Father was attached as honorary surgeon in Leicester, Mother was with the Red Cross, sister Viv in FANY driving army vehicles, Joan on social duties in her Peckham Settlement and John a ship's doctor.

My pianist boyfriend wrote that he was doing officer's training and here was I discovering that absence doesn't make the heart grow fonder! 'Out out of sight, out of mind' was more applicable to my situation for I

– wretch – was falling in love with another. The two of us were in a company of mostly European folk fleeing from Hitler's clutches and our Impresario was desperately trying to find contracts this side of the Atlantic. We soon learned that he had fixed a tour of South America in three weeks and until then we lodged in Greenwich Village, NY, where I lost my virginity to Jack.

Jack was brought up as a pacifist – as was his Father who had been jailed in the first war – and it was lucky that he could not patriotically return now to face a tribunal, though he did so later.

Summer 1940 – South America

Things were hotting up back home in England. The *Vollendamm*, the ship on which we had spent Christmas at sea, had been torpedoed by the Germans as it was bringing evacuee children over the Atlantic to safety. Londoners were taking mattresses down into the Underground tunnels to spend the nights away from the bombs.

My sister Joan in her Peckham Settlement was busy with the evacuations, *etc*. Brother John was starting to get his first surgical experience with wound dressings, and Jack's parents bought a tiny cottage for a hundred pounds on the banks of the River Tamar in Cornwall should refuge become necessary. So far the provinces had not been hit and America was still neutral.

Impresario Greanin had fixed a tour to start in Uruguay. So six of us English boarded a Grace Line ship, with our European dancer refugees and Jooss's Ballets, to cross the Equator for the first time.

Travelling also among the passengers was Toscanini and his orchestra, who were to give a concert in Rio on the way down. The ship docked at Rio for two days, and we were able to attend his concert and get our first impressions of South America. My only memories are of lamp-lit streets on the way to the concert hall and a rather muggy heat. We felt so thirsty that we bought lemonade from a street vendor and how delicious it was; only later were we warned of the ghastly diseases we would contract if we drank any liquids that had not been sterilised. In those days, the poor were even poorer than they are now and life in the smaller places seemed to us very primitive, with people dying of the plague, typhoid and other frightful diseases!

We enjoyed Toscanini's concert very much, but were aware of an uncanny atmosphere emanating from the platform. We did not know until later that the first violinist was a deputy for the usual man who had been killed in an accident that very day. Was the whole orchestra sending out its vibes to us?

Sociedad Pro-Arte Musical

JOOSS BALLET

Coreografía y producción de todos
los ballets de KURT JOOSS en
colaboración con AINO SIIMOLA

Dirección Artística: F. A. COHEN

En los pianos:
F. A. COHEN y F. P. WALDMAN

JUEVES 1o. DE FEBRERO
DE 1940 A LAS 5.30 P. M.

PROXIMOS CONCIERTOS:
JUSSI BJOERLING - Tenor
Miércoles 14 de Febrero
de 1940 a las 5.30 p. m.
BALLET de Pro-Arte, Marzo 4

Jooss Ballet – South America 1940

Next day, still in harbour, we were able to admire the sunny beauty of Rio. Why could we not, as Toscanini did, have performed in Rio the first time in passing instead of travelling all the way back again to dance? Looking at a map of South America, I am astounded at the enormous distances we covered by ship, boat, and train.

We went ashore at Santos after São Paulo and Jack and I found the most idyllic tropical bay with palm trees and yellow sand and not a soul in sight. We took photographs and had a delicious swim before returning to the boat.

When we set out for South America, our original Dartington Ballet was intact. German members were Fritz Cohen, our director, musical and otherwise; his wife and dancer Elsa; Twin or Fritz Waldmann and girl friend dancer Alida Mennen; Ernst Uthoff and Hungarian wife Lola Botka; Rudi Pescht who danced Death admirably with his great sturdy body; Rolf Alexander, the youngest male, trained in the Essen School since he was fourteen; comical little Heinz Schartz; Jack Gansert; Dutch Lukas Hoving; and Jack Skinner. The female dancers were English: Bunty Slack, Monica Johnston, and me; Ulla Soederbaum and Eva Leckstrom were both Swedish. Then there was Gabor Cossa, our busy little Hungarian Manager (later to open an antiques shop in Cambridge, and to gain fame with his Wigmore Hall 'recital' at the silent piano); Scotty whose name speaks for itself and who was our electrician-cum-everything-else, and Edith, our English wardrobe mistress, who had never dared to visit a dentist and in consequence often suffered with her remaining teeth!

As we left New York, we had had a letter from Kurt Jooss. He and Sigurd Leeder did not remain in internment very long – owing to influential bodies pulling strings I guess – and it seems that Jooss had every intention of joining us at some stage, having settled his wife and children now that Dartington had been taken over by the war office.

Jooss wrote:

> My dear Ladies & Boys,
> You must have grown so much since I last saw you that my typewriter refuses to print 'Kids' for you this time. Small wonder as more than a year has passed since we waved goodbye at Waterloo Station. What a year it was! I do not speak of Our sort of year: I now mean Yours. I am filled with unrestricted admiration, some sort of fatherly pride, when I think of the mountains of difficulties you have had in your way which have been victoriously overcome by your energy, initiative, team spirit

and faith. I know too that there may have been a great many minor catastrophies of which I did not hear. The daily setbacks and calamities which always tend to eat up one's energies that are so needed for the major tasks. I really do not want to make a sermon to you now; only to let you know that you are in my thoughts whilst learning of all these setbacks. Therefore I hope that, in spite of time and miles between us, we have not lost the inner contact and will understand one another quickly again as soon as circumstances allow us to meet again face to face and do new work together. There seems to be the need to repeat certain facts of importance which I have written in Cohen's letter. Let them please be known to everybody. I think it is good news altogether even if the results are not reached without a good deal of pain and there will certainly be more of it before we spend our summer together and do our new productions. Let's be full of hope and confidence for the future, and at the same time let me thank you for all you have done for the common cause and especially the good spirits whose collaboration has made this possible, Greanin and Cossa. It seems that the Ballet Jooss spirit is able to shine in the dark and have a guiding light. You know I cannot promise you anything at this moment but certainly our plans are good. Let us try and make the best of them.

Jack and I were horrified when we all sat down to a communal meal in the hotel; plates piled with almost the whole of a cut-up cow were put in front of us, and not a single vegetable in sight. This was the dry land of cactus and we vegetarians were in for a bad time. Fortunately, we were able to find quite nice milk bars in Buenos Aires, where one could order omelettes and cheese dishes, followed by arroz con leche, Jack's favourite sweet! And how ultra-sweet their cookies were; dulce de leche was sicklier than a tin of English condensed milk!

The highlight of that particular trip was when we returned to Rio and had a week's holiday before travelling west again. There the theatre, as in most of the big towns, was large and old fashioned. Jack and I, who were always together when possible, had found a dressing room on a top floor where we were able to cook most of our meals. By this time Jack, always resourceful, had fitted up an ingenious suitcase containing pots and pans and cooking arrangements! We even bought a tent, hired a little boat, and set off to explore the beautiful bays round Rio, landing up at Ipanema Beach where we pitched the tent. The next morning we walked a short distance to a shack restaurant for some sustenance. How trusting we were. On our return the travelling rug, the camera and other things had vanished, though we had been sitting eating only a few yards away.

The audiences were mostly very enthusiastic and in the larger places the bookings were good. As we were on a British Council tour, there were many rather formal invitations to parties after the show. Often, the performance didn't start until nearly nine o'clock at night and we all felt too tired to climb into respectable attire and be on our best behaviour.

The first part of the trip over to the West was made along narrow primitive roads in a bus that had seen better days and was certainly not used to carrying a company with very heavy theatre equipment. It took ten hours to reach the little station where a crowded train would carry us through the

Jack in Ball in Old Vienna

Andes to Chile. We passed through poverty-stricken hamlets with scattered homemade huts belonging to ragged-looking peasants whose males wore great black trilby-like hats – even a little boy had one almost over his eyes.

The scenery became greener as we approached the mountains and started to climb to the station. Then – what scenery! Never before had I seen such majestic mountains. No matter that there was standing room only on the little train; I stood on the observation platform and gazed up at the snowy cloak of Aconcagua.

We were a very compatible company sharing this gypsy life in what we often felt were rather dangerous circumstances as time wore on. When we returned to the larger towns we were not such a novelty for the box office and our finances grew stretched, but we were a democratic company; our director held regular meetings with us to discuss our budget and future plans. Everyone was granted his or her fare home and any salary owing, as later we had to go on half pay! The necessary funds for this were laid aside as we went along, and so far I had found that I could live quite satisfactorily.

Our situation was worrying, though there was far more to worry about when we received the war news from home. Jack seriously contemplated returning to England and Monica and Gert Malgrem did manage to catch a boat back over the Atlantic safely. Owing to the restricted finances our trip back to Rio had to be made in the steerage class of a Brazilian boat called *Duc de Cachias*. We were packed into stuffy little cabins holding four people, water seeping through the deck boards on to our bunks. There were animals travelling in the stern behind us, chickens and sheep, one of which we called Suzy. One day we noticed, as we walked the decks, that Suzy had disappeared. When, soon after, the number of chickens began to dwindle, how glad Jack and I were to be vegetarians!

Jack had a top bunk in his cabin and told us he was awoken at dawn by something sitting on his chest – a rat. There was more excitement when a group of us were bathing off a Brazilian beach and a squad of police descended, seized Lukas, our Dutchman, and carted him off to jail. It seemed his bathing pants were too brief for respectability. Fortunately our manager was able to retrieve him in time for the performance that night.

Jooss never did come and join us, bringing other ballets from the repertoire as we had hoped, and our future depended on the advance efforts of Greanin to book us up the Pacific side of the continent, and on the efforts of our Dutch Manager Rymsdyke in the USA. He was working through the Schubert Theatres agency and told us of a probable ten-week tour up there again with probably Mexico to follow. Alas, it never materialised, but our spirits rose at the time.

I consulted my diary to remind me of our travels on the West side of South America, opening the pages at 19 October 1940. I read: 'Italy has invaded Greece. Jack has written to our director Cohen warning him that, when it is possible to get transport, he would like to return home'; also that we had experienced an earthquake in Santiago, given a charity performance and been given a cocktail party by the British Council.

The thought of Jack leaving saddened me, and I hoped he would not be able to obtain transport but things were looking up as regards theatre dates. The Santiago Municipal managed the theatres in most important towns up the coast, and we would then be bound for Peru and Columbia. We had to have many rehearsals, as always some member of the cast had jaundice, gastric troubles or strained muscles, necessitating a complicated juggling around of roles. But it was warm and summerlike and the sea in Valparaiso was of the deepest blue, making up for the drainage systems which left much to be desired, and the flea population sharing our beds – very trying! We left Chile by boat on 20 November stopping at several ports on the way where we often went ashore. It was the first time I actually floated on the Pacific Ocean – and I imagine the last – gazing at bare mountains along the coastline most of the way. The ship was of a better class than the old *Duc de Cachias* although we did carry racehorses bound for New York in the hold!

I shared a cabin with Swedish Eva and a friend of Cohen's and there was a considerable swell as we left Vina Del Mar. Eva alas, having eaten too much doubtful food before embarkation, was violently sick on the first part of the journey. She seemed very ill and I could do nothing for her, which was most worrying.

The wall of barren mountains which formed the coastline was indeed most impressive seen from the boat. We were told there was never rainfall up there which accounted for the peasants' huts mostly being built of bamboo sticks and standing on chicken-like legs to let the draught in!

We reached Lima in five days with Eva fortunately recovered. The town had recently had a very bad earthquake which had killed a large number of people. The buildings we saw, though not impressive, were most attractive in spite of the damage. We were again at a large Municipal Theatre, where we were to spend Christmas.

In spite of a lot of us suffering from gastric troubles, we were lucky enough to make an expedition to Inca territory. There were no guardians in the ancient graveyard of Patchakamac, and Jack came away with an old vase and a black lock of Inca hair.

We left Peru, and called in at many smaller places on the coast of Ecuador on our way to Colombia, where we went by bus from Cali up to the thin high air of Bogotá for a month, staying with European families. Jack and I were with a couple called Wieseltier. He was a sharp little fellow and she cooked us the hardest and most indigestible omelettes we had ever tasted. She must have put more flour than egg in them; fortunately we had very little appetite at that high altitude. In fact, Jack spent most of the time when not at the theatre ill in bed, as did others of the company after excursions to explore the rural peasant dwellings at even higher altitudes.

Whether Jack's health or the knowledge of the difficulty of getting a passage back to England had changed his mind, he informed Cohen that he would stay on – to everybody's relief as, if our numbers continued to dwindle, we would eventually be stranded. Fortunately, we were able to recruit a male dancer from the National Company of Uruguay, a short stocky man called Alfredo Corvino. We named him 'Botcho'; he had a good technique and was a friendly little fellow.

We then went by bus to Caracas, where we stayed outside the town in a large house standing in a courtyard, where mango trees grew behind a sort of hut allotted to me and Jack. Jack's watercolour of those trees, though somewhat faded, hangs on the wall of his workshop still.

Here we made friends with English folk working for Shell Oil who took Bunty and me for picnics on idyllic palm-treed beaches – looking just like a holiday brochure.

This was the last stop on our tour; our contract was finished and it was not long before we were to catch a boat back to New York. Some of the group elected to remain in South America: Rudi Pesht, and the Uthoffs who would later return to Santiago to direct the Municipal Ballet.

It was exciting to be going back to New York even though our future was precarious. Our manager had procured work for us at the Schubert Theatre sharing with a Gilbert and Sullivan show. *HMS Pinafore* was the first half, and we presented *Green Table* after the interval. It must have seemed the most extraordinary mixture in entertainment to any audience.

In spite of telegrams despatched to the consulate in Caracas from influential people such as Anthony Eden, Cordell Hull and Dorothy Elmhurst, someone at our end had seemed determined to delay our visas on account of the Germans among us – this, in spite of the fact that we now learnt that we were to give a performance up in Montreal for the English Air Raid Relief Fund. A telegram from the Mayor of Plymouth who could vouch for the standing of Dartington on our behalf seemed finally to settle the difficulties which could have been even more severe when America decided to declare war, as was expected at any day now.

By this time Crete had been invaded and, on Palm Sunday, Yugoslavia. No wonder our Jewish and European members hoped to find theatre jobs in America before England was swallowed up too. Eventually, we left for New York on the *Santa Paula*. We were now in such financial straits that once again we had to travel steerage in hot little cabins. At a meeting held before leaving we learned that we would now be living on royalties borrowed from our pianists who had composed most of our music, and that our manager Greanin had been trying to borrow money in New York. I did know that he had contacted the parents of my brother's friend there and arranged that three of us might stay with them while rehearsing.

But the trip was not too uncomfortable and I remember sleeping quite happily on the deck in the hammock we bought in the same market as our Panama hats. The ship docked long enough to get ashore at Portocabello, a beautiful little place so named, we were told, as a ship could be secure from any gales, moored with only a strand of fine hair in this very sheltered harbour. We were also able to spend time ashore in Bermuda, the atmosphere seeming so clear after Caracas.

New York again

After a few nights in a rather second-class hotel with the ballet we all found – to my relief – very cheap but satisfactory accommodation in Greenwich Village; the owners, as had most New Yorkers, having escaped from the summer heat of the city. We were to pay $4 a week and would

receive $8 a week as soon as we started work again.

'Work' meant rehearsals to replace the gaps left in ballets by members who had forsaken us or were ill. Many of us were suffering from stomach troubles and Heinz Scharze, known as Pipsy, was found to be suffering from typhoid. When this was diagnosed we all had to be tested to see if we were carriers; fortunately no one was.

There were still two months before performances were in sight but we were saved by Agnes de Mille's request to compose a new Ballet for us. This was called *Drum Sound from Hackensack* and was based on the lore of Dutch

Jack in Drum Sound from Hackensack

settlers. Jack was a fine figure as an American Indian chief, and Ulla Soederbaum a charming heroine. The whole thing was a great success as first number on the programme at the Maxime Elliott Theatre with Ballets Jooss following it. The show got an excellent review in the *New York Times* and other papers and we played to full houses, stealing the ballet audiences from other theatres in New York.

In a letter to the Uthoffs, now in charge of the ballet in Santiago, I wrote: 'It is hardly our style but Ulla, coached to dance the chief role as Agnes would

Joy in Drum Sound from Hackensack

have danced it herself, makes an excellent job of being successfully dramatic in her naïvely childish way. She is the only serious character in the ballet. The rest one might term American-type slapstick as the audience laughs just as it would watching Laurel and Hardy. The rest of the girls are Red Indian premonitions, in black wigs, tights and loincloths and are hardly serious, though meant to be.'

We had taken on new dancers to fill the gaps made by the several deserters, though it was difficult to find suitable men. Classes, rehearsals and new choreography continued as we still looked forward to the dates which our sponsors had guaranteed. Jooss cabled that he was still awaiting a visa in order to join us, bringing Sigurd Leeder and some female dancers with him.

We did two more weeks of performances. Japan attacked Pearl Harbour and America declared war just about the time Jooss's boat passage to join us was booked.

We learned later that the Elmhursts, as well as our musicians and manager, had been keeping us alive financially and soon we all started to feel the pinch while endeavouring to fix passages back home.

Finally I had to borrow one hundred dollars from my brother's friend's parents. Their son Tollie had enlisted in the Royal Canadian Air Force and was shortly to transfer to England where he would visit my home. We now had an invitation to stay at their house in 61st Street which we accepted, saying that we would help in any way they wished. As it happened, Tollie's mother was an interior decorator and I was able to draw some of her designs for her. Later, when her Finnish servant couple left Jack and I took over the running of the house and I acted as cook.

These were happy times when one dismissed thoughts of guilt for not sharing the war fever at home. The Bells had been very kind and invited us and ballet to the cool, country atmosphere of Brookville.

Mrs Bell, or Louise as she preferred to be, had two sons by her first husband Toll Taylor; Toll and Read. Toll was the Cambridge friend of my brother, and in the forces, while Read was very anti-war. He lived in the Bells' house at Brookville, had a girl friend, and we felt that he rather resented his mother's kindness to us. She, however, adored Tollie – who was definitely the favourite son – and, therefore, any family in England that he attached himself to. She must have felt that she was reciprocating in America on his behalf.

From time to time, my Mother hinted in her letters that she would be very averse to me marrying into any of these arty circles who inhabited Dartington Hall and in one letter she ventured to enquire if my relationship with Jack was more than platonic! Of course, by this time it was and Louise guessed this, and that we should share the engagement party she was giving for Read and his girlfriend. We agreed to save her from further embarrassment from friends, though we ourselves felt very embarrassed at such etiquette. Did she tell my mother, I wonder, of this decision?

Louise's family knew, or was related to, the Drapers. Ruth Draper was well known as a Joyce Grenfell type of humorous performer; we saw one of her shows and one of Paul Draper's with his virtuoso tapping to classical music. Whenever I could escape from house or secretarial duties, I would sneak off to ballet class given by a Mme Ivanzova, a highlight of the day. Madame, every now and then, would pass through our midst carrying a tiny watering can with which she sprayed the floor at our feet, so that we would not slip, a ritual that was new to me and never forgotten. Nor do I forget Jack and I pitching our little tent above the Hudson River in the State Park, cooking omelette and peas over a small stove before sleeping there the night, undisturbed by any Yogi Bear that was supposed to live there!

Finally, whether it was as a result of Jack knowing someone in the British Embassy, or someone else's influence, Bunty, Jack and I were able to board a freighter in New York Harbour bound for home. We must have been somewhat haggard in appearance. We had been exactly a year in the States working very hard, attending ballet classes as well as housekeeping. I had had a baby aborted, and Jack had had his tonsils out.

It was 6 June 1942; we mixed with a motley crowd on board and had to share cabins with a collection of odd types. One inmate of Jack's cabin

Jack and Joy's engagement, New York 1942

was an old Jewish fellow determined to get back to be buried beside his wife, should the war finish him off. Strangely enough, he might never have had that wish granted. We sat in Halifax harbour for an annoyingly long time while other ships gathered to make a convoy. Then, not far out into the Atlantic, the ships' sirens sounded and depth charges boomed under us. Had it not been for Jack's endeavours to dress the old man and get him on deck he might have had a stroke there and then, and ended in a watery grave.

We were lucky, but another boat in our convoy was torpedoed. Fortunately the crew was all rescued and the ship was towed back to Halifax. But how I shivered after the danger was over; I could hardly wait to get below to relieve myself! Strange what effect one's nerves have on such an occasion!

All the male passengers on that trip were required to do two-hour watches on deck and fortunately we reached Liverpool by the end of June without mishap, and thence home to our families after nearly three years' absence.

Cambridge 1942

Mother's eyes lit up at the sight of the fruit Louise Bell had sent home with me. Oranges were like gold in wartime England and she made a large jar of marmalade out of one grapefruit. There was a letter awaiting me from the RAF Station at Linton-on-Ouse: 'I regret to advise you PO Taylor was reported missing on the night of 6 June 1942 and a cable has been sent to his Mother to this effect'.

Poor Louise; she never gave up hope, even visiting France hopefully for information at the end of hostilities. She opened her home to servicemen on leave in New York as her husband was abroad on government war service. She wrote to us later about an Australian fellow who grew pineapples in peacetime with whom she eventually emigrated. He must have resembled son Tollie in some motherloving way! She took to writing Australian history amongst the pineapples and we corresponded until her death.

Meanwhile, Jooss had written to Bunty, Jack and me that he was re-forming the Ballet in Cambridge and rehearsals should start in August. By this time, Jack had met my mother and been his useful self to her in Leicester, and I had visited his parents in Harrow. My mother still entreated me, however, to be sensible and leave this arty existence and partner, blaming herself for my Dresden and Dartington training, at the same time causing me to feel an utterly ungrateful cad for all my parents' love. Jack's Mother was satisfied with our union as long as we were not living in sin as she did not approve of the girlfriend he had forsaken – who was now, incidentally, recruited into the Ballet from Jooss's school in Cambridge.

We knew, however, that it was highly unlikely that Jack would be able to continue with Jooss as he now was due to go before the conscientious objectors' tribunal. We women dancers were all exempt from military call-up as we were to perform in factories round England under the auspices of CEMA. the Council for the Encouragement of Music and the Arts.

Doctor Alice Roughton was a psychiatrist at Addenbrooke's Hospital who lived in Cambridge; she was an extremely kind philanthropist to artists and students and had taken Jooss and the Ballet under her wing. She and other influential folk had arranged for us to be housed on King's Parade very near the Arts Theatre. We dancers started to clean up and furnish the accommodation, using Sigurd Leeder's and Jooss's furniture. Sigurd was to live there but Jooss and family already occupied an annexe to the Roughtons' house at 9 Adams Road.

Letter from Kurt Jooss to his old retainers 8 July 1942:

Dear Joy, Bunty and Jack.

This I write in a great hurry and therefore would you please pass the letter round between yourselves in order to save time, as I have no typewriter with me. I just got word from CEMA for you. 'Will you instruct every individual member of the Ballet to tell the local labour exchange that he is "employed by CEMA". This applies if he is changing his occupation or is called up for National Service. In the latter case inform me at once and I [Miss Glasgow, the acting secretary] will send him the appropriate forms to fill in by way of application for his deferment.' So much for what you'll have to do for your registration.

Thank you so much for your letters, let me explain to you later what our new organisation is going to be in detail: today only a few words.

Contrary to what I had intended to do at the beginning, namely organise a 'Chamber Ballet', we will build a new 'Ballets Jooss' as a full sized company together with the restaging of the old repertoire in its main items and make some new ballets and hope to start performing in January a tour under CEMA auspices combined with a normal tour as we know it and in collaboration with the Cambridge Arts Theatre. Finances will come from CEMA and Cambridge friends. Our board of directors will be Higgins of the Arts Theatre, Dr Alice Roughton, a representative from CEMA, Professor Dent and myself. We shall be a non-profit-making company and though connected luckily to CEMA, virtually independent. There will probably be some legal business in order to clear up the question of former and future ownership and responsibility for debts incurred by the previous company. This is being looked into and we will probably have information in a few days.

As to the beginning of work it seems advisable to start in the beginning days of August. I will let you know about this when I see how things are going at Cambridge early next week.

I, personally shall finish my work with Sadlers Wells which has nothing to do with our Ballet. It is for the production of The Magic Flute. I will be going back for a new production for them in October for about seven weeks. It should be possible for Ballet work in that time not to be held up.

Let that be all for today and let's hope the others will soon arrive safely as you did.

Kind regards.

Yours

Kurt Jooss.

Excerpt from mother's letter on reforming of Ballets Jooss and Joy's participation in Cambridge:

I know that brown Lavatory paper; they brought some to the depot some time ago. I expect when my stock is exhausted I shall have to buy some. I am amazed that Monica has been released from nursing and am glad you are eating well and have put on weight. John says you have something wrong with your kidneys. Why not consult Dr Roughton?

Darling, both your letters ended in the same theme, and much as I desire not to enter into argument, I must point out, that your presence was not disturbing. It is always hungered for by your poor little ordinary Mama and she was pained to the utmost when you hurried away. You should remember how little we have had of you since you were left on Dresden Railway station all those years ago.

There your statement of no longer being the child who fitted so well into the scheme of things rather falls to pieces as it has always been your scheme and not ours, hasn't it dear? We have never said you 'nay' from the beginning, and much against our judgment, let you go your own way, asking nothing but love and one promise from you in return. The love I know you have given, the promise, I fear you mean to break. My opposition is for your ultimate good. You are, as you say, old enough to choose for yourself which I agree but consider that you have not explored and weighed things as a mature person would. You have taken on an impression which has taken three years to fix itself in your imagination. Give it a chance to clear itself I beg of you for the sake of any children you might have in the future and don't plunge into things.

For myself: whether you are in your little bed upstairs, in the USA or Cambridge, I am always thinking of you. I feel rather like the musical box doll you danced at the Wigman School. My spring has broken so that I keep going on dancing for you all, and the joy of being has snapped. My pride in you has been so great and I have lived for your happiness. John says it has aged me and I know it has. He says I am foolish to take it to heart and should just laugh at you and tell you if you want to make a damn fool of yourself, to do so and let it rest there. I wish I could, but unfortunately I can't, I love you too much. I am not going to say any more about it, you will please yourself I have no doubt; I have done my utmost. You have never savoured an uncertain background or the miseries of insecurity. Life, or shall we say Daddy, has always made things too easy for you.

Reading these letters of the past tears at my heart and yet I do not remember it doing so in those days, nor the guilty conscience I must have had – and how selfish I must have seemed to displease my parents to such an extent! They had allowed and afforded the training and even mentioned being proud of their offending offspring. Mama had enjoyed her visit to the beautiful city of Dresden in the thirties, and meeting Mary Wigman and her sister Elisabeth who had auditioned me. She had also seen how gracious Dartington was in its surroundings, in spite of later referring to its inhabitants as 'an arty crowd' in a derogatory way – in those days, a way of life described as 'Bohemian.'.

Jack's parents found it a struggle to provide a theatre training on a journalist's salary; they were familiar with the Bohemian way of life, and were only too keen on Jack's prowess in the theatre world. They were also not averse to my union with Jack as long as we were decently married.

There could be no argument for either of us escaping the draft as we were working for the British Government officially now, and I could tell my parents that we were sponsored by influential and respected Cambridge citizens. Later, after Jack's tribunal hearings, Alice Roughton was responsible for procuring his duties as a porter locally at Addenbrooke's Hospital from where he could be called on when urgently needed in the company, as was sometimes possible when a venue was close. In September I wrote to an American friend of the peaceful beauty of Cambridge with its old buildings and the church we looked out on to from our attic window. Such a tranquil setting made it difficult to believe that not far away men were killing one another.

As far as my mother's grief over my choice of Jack as a partner was concerned, could I have softened the blow earlier by warning her in my correspondence from America of our increasing attachment to one another? Perhaps I was cowardly, but I knew she did not live in the same atmosphere, socially or artistically, as I had become accustomed to and though I hoped she was reconciled by now to a working dancer as a daughter, the idea of a dancer son-in-law she had not yet set eyes upon would be abhorrent! How could she tell her friends? The Dance to them was not a profession for a man! And were not the most famous male practitioners of the Arts, possessing both female and male characteristics, homosexuals?

Oddly enough, Jack's athleticism and his Margaret Morris training and acting experience made him more of an artist than a dancer; very suitable for Jooss's company whose dancers alas had seldom the virtuoso type of ballet technique as those trained in the classical school.

9 Adams Road

Cambridge

21/7/43

Dear Joy,

Though full rehearsals will begin on August 4th only, could you manage to come here as soon as possible? We are doing some preparatory work and would be very glad to have you for it. Any day from now would be all right and we can accommodate you for the time being at 9 Adams Road. With kind regards.

Yours sincerely,

Kurt Jooss

When I received the letter from Jooss bidding me to attend rehearsals I left Leicester before Jack departed from Harrow, where he was staying with his parents. I had had a letter from Jack from which I quote: 'I hate being so unfilial, but give me my hermit life any time.' As he was their only child, to escape to Cambridge was as unkind a deed as was mine. His mother did come there later instead of visiting their cottage in Cornwall having heard that the young man who was renting it had walked over the edge of the quay one dark night and drowned in the River Tamar which ran along the end of the road. She had meant to prepare the place for him before his arrival. Poor fellow, he was to have wed in a fortnight.

In March 1943 the Ballets Jooss left Cambridge with a partly new cast on an English tour starting up North where we had our first view of German air raid destruction, especially in Liverpool. How lucky it was that the city's cathedral had escaped bomb damage though surrounded by charred buildings.

Jack was to go to Addenbrooke's Hospital in Cambridge in about four weeks, and was to be replaced by Angelo Rovida, who had stayed behind in South America. Angelo had managed to board a ship in a convoy and, amazingly enough, the ship docked in Liverpool while we were there. Angelo told us that they had had to go all round the Cape and had lost ten ships on the way.

Jack in Prodigal Son; *to his right is Ulla Soederbaum*

Jack had still time before returning to Cambridge to perform in Scotland with us. He was now dancing the Old Soldier in *Green Table* and the Father in *Prodigal Son*.

How green and beautiful it all seemed after only English towns, and how friendly the people! Margaret Morris and Ferguson had moved the school

Jack as the Old Soldier

from Chelsea to Glasgow We had many visitors backstage and we were all invited to their homes.

A considerable time elapsed before the Ballet was able to occupy the house at 13 King's Parade. Jack spent much time helping with the furnishing when Jooss and Leeder claimed their borrowed furniture back. While working at Adden-brooke's Hospital, Jack acted as landlord to the students who lodged there during the next Jooss tour away.

His letters of that time show what energy he expended – hospital duty, warden for the lodgings on KP, secretary by post for the Ballets Jooss manager, and making handbags in company with a friend and fellow worker at the hospital, Donald Dale, to augment their slender salaries. Donald was a slightly eccentric fellow with a penchant for vintage cars. When petrol became available, he would drive up to the main entrance of the hospital in his 4$^{1}/_{2}$-litre Bentley and pick Jack up after work to the amazement of the hall porter. They would drive to Donald's house where Donald, with the help of a very talented schoolboy son, had set up a workshop in the attic to make leather handbags, most likely of old leather car seats retrieved from a scrap yard! Their industry augmented their slender wartime salaries; I wonder how many retired dancers and nurses still have those attractive shoulder bags? I certainly have one still stowed away in my cupboard. It definitely kept Jack's hand in for the clever props he was to make in the future, for the act of Emerson & Jayne.

It seems Jack and Donald were very popular with all the staff in the hospital. Jack wrote of the 'Egg Nurse' who took a fancy to him with frequent gifts of eggs which, then rationed, were a great prize. We were always frank in our letters to each other and I learnt that when he finally succumbed to her advances, he decided she was not his type. Luckily she left soon after. His other adventure apparently was with the attractive

Donald Dale (right) and his family – a picture taken by Jack Skinner

painter wife of another friend, an optician, also doing his war work in Addenbrooke's – he later cared most admirably for our eyes until we lived in different towns. With all this activity, Jack never got enough sleep, being the active soul he was, supposedly with a heart murmur. Being a vegetarian and a non-smoker with a strong body, he should have lived to as ripe an old age as Bernard Shaw did but alas, his talents and inventiveness kept him too active.

His letters to me on tour were seldom in sad vein. Some of the time, he stayed comfortably with the Roughtons in the very friendly atmosphere. So many visitors, artists and students gathered there; how much our dear, generous Alice Roughton enjoyed all this humanity around her!

There were often CEMA performances in the town. A show was put on by Stephen Spender, Peggy Ashcroft and a pianist. Jack commented that Spender could sing very well but was very bad at reading his verse; Peggy Ashcroft read his verse beautifully but couldn't sing!

Alice Roughton would often have Sunday evening gatherings of Cambridge notabilities, concerts, *etc* in the large room at the back of the house when it wasn't full of mattresses for the likes of us wayfarers.

It was nearing Christmas 1943 and Jack and I spent time with our respective parents. Both my mother and I kept off the subject of my relationship with Jack – she was still agonising at the thought of acquiring a dancer as a son-in-law, I not daring to tell her that she would have to.

My sister was also visiting home at the time and I confided in her that I might be pregnant, as my period had not arrived on time which was most unusual, causing me to consult Alice Roughton before I left Cambridge. She of course, knowing Jack and myself by now, had strongly recommended that we married. This we did in the Cambridge Shire Hall with Alice, Bunty and Monica as witnesses, the only people apart from my family who knew about our marriage. Later, I was to receive the most heart-rending letters from Mama on the subject.

The tragedy reflected on her rather than on myself. Could it have been because she herself had forsaken home for a nursing profession, married the first consultant Leicester surgeon around at the time and felt she must not shock the circles she moved in? Thank heavens that when Jack and I were able to visit Leicester, as we did regularly later, she realised she had gained in Jack the most favourite and useful of her sons-in-law. He was soon popular with all her friends,

After Christmas I was back in Cambridge to rehearse for two new ballets which had to be finished for late January in the Arts Theatre. Also, after obtaining an address from a gynaecologist in London, the demise of junior. How could one trail an infant around as circus people do, should one want to give it a trade other than a dancer's? *Pandora* was having teething troubles and the rehearsals were tedious. Papa Jooss was irritable and had reason to be so with so many changes in our cast. Monica and Bunty had both left to get married, Monica to a childhood friend from the past, and Bunty to her Shell Oil friend she'd met in Venezuela. Maya our Swiss dancer was unsatisfied with the roles she was given and was about to leave; others had remained in America and the new members were unaccustomed to our technique and Jooss–Leeder schooling.

It was hard work, as it seemed that everyone had to appear in every scene, of which there were many. Again, as in *Green Table*, the ballet was intended to portray a moral message, Noelle as *Pandora* releasing it from the box. I remember Hein Heckroth's monster costumes looking most horrendous; to say the least, they were rather uncomfortable to wear. Jooss himself played the main monster. At the same time Hans Zullig was choreographing *Le Bosquet,* a light ballet to music by Rameau. We were clad in delightful costumes by Doris Zinkeisen and photographs were taken of us posing as a picture by Watteau. *Pandora,* after a Cambridge début, received rather mixed notices.

CEMA – separation.

From Cambridge, we set off for Oxford on the tour of factories for CEMA. I had to leave my dear Jack behind in charge of the bins and corpses, as well as 13 King's Parade.

I remember feeling really ill with flu one night on a rather hard palliasse in a stable-like dormitory with the rest of the ballet in Kidderminster. I don't think we actually performed in factories; rather that the workers came to see us in some outer building or hall.

It must have been a relief to my mother when, at the end of the war, our company donned khaki uniforms and set off for the continent. Life had been so awkward when I had returned home from the USA in the company of a conscientious objector, for she and her friends met almost daily at the Red Cross war depot. Sister Joan had written how, in London, some basements of bombed buildings were often turned into water reservoirs and how many of her children evacuees often had lice. I knew then what war could do to the mind by hearing someone's retort 'Give them to the COs' (conscientious objectors).

ENSA

Clad in our officers' khaki we had left Cambridge early in January 1945 for London where we were to spend a night in a large building which had been turned into a transit camp. Males were strictly segregated from females of course, which later on was rather sad for our married couples! Now that I live not far from Folkestone and look down to the sea over The Leas, I recognise the building that was the next camp – where we were to spend time waiting to catch a boat to Calais. Good gracious – it's over fifty years ago and its still there, old and ugly at the back, in contrast to the fairground in front.

From Calais to Ostend in a hard-seated bus, after two days' delay through a devastated Dunkerque and many cups of NAAFI tea, we reached Belgium, where we were to entertain the first troops.

The shops seemed so much better stocked here at the end of the war than did the English ones, especially food shops. They had just received their first consignment of oranges, and we gloried in the rich cakes available. As for the performances we gave, on not very suitable stages, it was clear that the soldiers would much rather have been entertained by a row of topless Tiller girls!

We were to return as civilian performers after this tour, and as I had not visited Belgium with Mary Wigman's group earlier and Belgium was new to me, we were able to savour excellent civilian audiences as well as more luscious cakes; also Bruxelles Grand Place with its crooked tower. We were most impressed on being told that when the architect discovered this shocking builder's mistake he clambered to the top of it and flung himself to his death. Could this have been true?

Sometimes, as at the first stop in Germany, we had only very small audiences and saw pathetic sights of shivering German soldiers with army blankets round their shoulders, incarcerated in PoW camps intended previously for the British. They looked half starved, and there were we, being fed on real butter! How pleased the German folk were to receive our English white bread instead of their pale grey version. Reaching Münster, we were driven straight to the garrison theatre which was surrounded by some most imposing buildings; we learnt that these had once housed the Luftwaffe, but were now inhabited by British soldiers – and, for the time being, by us.

We were certainly doing our war work, though somewhat late. Members of the company started to sicken in different ways owing to the awkward housing conditions, the cold and the strange food. Often we found windows part open to the icy weather, and doors broken in by our troops, as the Germans had left their army quarters intact until they had been forced out. It was usual for ENSA artistes to be accommodated in the broken-down hostels, not always near the theatre. Owing to sickness, therefore, programmes were constantly juggled around and only the ballets with small casts were presented. Jooss himself, though healthy, must have been happy to return to the fatherland, and he absented himself to search for his past – or at least what remained of it.

Jack wrote:

> TO HIS WIFE
> (After the Manner of the Chinese)
>
> In the morning I rose at seven;
> For half the day I worked in the big hospital.
> Back at home I found you had already gone.
> Miserably I put myself to bed.
> My heart thumps, my body aches,
> My thoughts jangle and spin.
> The food you prepared is turning black.
> Soon the flowers will be dead.
> I shall not see you for three months.
> Would I could sleep till then.

Jack continually regaled me with such tit bits and tales of life at Addenbrooke's. Night duty was not always less unpleasant or exhausting; he described how a lunatic he was called to one night thought his room was a lift which went up and down and would crash any moment. The man had all the buttons off Jack's coat while he held him down and after about nine and half hours nonstop, Jack hardly knew which one of them was the madder.

Cambridge nevertheless was a pleasant town in which to live – not always the hermit life he claimed, judging from the attention he received from various nurses. Many good plays visited the Arts Theatre, and there were concerts and recitals. Benjamin Britten had just finished *Peter Grimes* and one could enjoy films such as *Brief Encounter* with Leslie Howard and Celia Johnson and in summer Jack rode out in the country on his old moped – or 'pop-pop' as we called it – even as far as Newmarket.

ENSA continued

We learned that the Ballets Rambert had had a far more successful and interesting tour than ours, but realised that they had been sent on a circuit of more civilised towns. Even Beatrice Lehman, who had preceded us, had gathered an audience of only twenty and had refused to play.

On one occasion we had even fewer; Jooss was still absent in Essen but Gabor Cossa, deputising for him, refused to do the same! My diary of the time cruelly says: 'We would have danced to only half a soldier'!

The hostels were not always dilapidated; indeed we were often housed in comfortable surroundings, later attended by poverty-stricken Germans such as a chambermaid shuffling around in her last pair of holed slippers, and waiters and stagehands forced into a black market. They would come along with penknives and pathetic little trinkets, hoping to swop them for our NAAFI cigarettes, which they then resold. We heard their butter ration was only a quarter of a pound a week, sugar half a pound a month, supplemented only by swapping with cigarettes. I, as a vegetarian, didn't feed too well on NAAFI food and relied partly on the dried egg Jack sent from his English rations.

We went up to play the Stadtsspielhaus in Hamburg where Herman Mendt had returned at the start of war, having then been Ballets Jooss stage manager, and his wife our wardrobe mistress. They entertained us at their home. Little did I know that Jack and I, as Emerson & Jayne, would fly our Magic Carpet many times in future years at the Hansa-Theater almost next door.

As we travelled deeper into Germany the audiences grew larger and more appreciative. Brussels, then wonderful Paris! Even though war weary it was beautiful; I had never known it properly for when I was with Mary Wigman we had only played Germany and Scandinavia.

We performed at the Théatre des Champs Elysées after a press conference, where we drank too many glasses of champagne. It was a wonder any of the dancers kept upright on the stage – but we must somehow have remained vertical, urged on by 'Bravos!' We took many curtains that night and had full houses the whole week. Paris will have remembered the

Noelle de Mosa as Pandora

success of *Green Table* when it won first prize for the most original composition in a competition at the Concours International de Choréographie in 1932.

We met Dmitri Bouchène once again; he had designed the many sumptuous costumes for *Prodigal Son* and *Chronica*. He insisted we go to a play one night starring Jouvet whom we visited afterwards in his dressing room. We also went and sat in the gallery of the Chatelet another time for twenty francs to see *La Folle de Chatelaine* from which I can only remember a fine actress, whose name I cannot recall, sitting in her chair in a large room hung with curtains and cobwebs!

We went on to good audiences at the Monneau Theatre in Brussels but not before Cossa had had his trunk stolen from the corridor of the train en route. The train must have been infested with fleas, as Noelle de Mosa and I got attacked in the night and had to appear on stage the next day with swollen eyes that were difficult to cover with makeup, and gave us a pig-like appearance!

Thence to Scandinavia and Holland, where I received the joyful news that Jack's number had come up for release from national service. He would be joining the Company on the next tournée which we learned would be to the USA again.

The Last Jooss Tour

In the meantime, it was back to Cambridge to regroup. A few dancers were leaving. Pat Clogstoun had decided to marry her officer boyfriend, reunited in Paris. Noelle de Mosa had married Rolf Alexander but they were fortunately still with us and returned with us all to Cambridge. I gave in my notice at the same time as Yoma Sassburg, neither of us wanting a further long separation from our husbands. Yoma and I stayed for the following English tour. One seldom earned praise from Papa Jooss but when one brought about a difficult situation, such as handing in one's notice, it was suspiciously unconvincing to hear how well one now suddenly danced in *Seven Heroes*, and the

Rolf Alexander

Young Girl in *Green Table*. Yoma was also told she should now dance the part of *Pandora;* Noelle, said Jooss now, was too sweet and delicate a dancer for this forceful role.

Before we set off on another trip to the USA, Jooss had announced that Jack would most likely be joining us soon. I wrote to Jack to cheer him up, telling him how important he must be to Jooss. He must have been worn out acting as secretary and welfare agent for ballet requirements by post, in addition to running the hostel at 13 King's Parade where everyone hoped to return for the forthcoming rehearsal period. He was actually having to search elsewhere in Cambridge to house everyone, in addition to his tiring hospital duties and the growing handbag venture.

The Jooss Company had by this time recruited several new members from the School and other companies, some totally unaccustomed to the Laban technique, making rehearsals long and tiring. A session with the Soldiers in the brothel scene of *Green Table* seemed endless, so long did it take them to master the various lifts. It was extremely wearing.

Moreover, these male dancers were earning far more than we original members of the Company. Monica Johnston's salary was the same as mine – only seven pounds a week! We considered this totally unfair and I wrote to Jooss accordingly; I cannot remember his reply.

Life once again became a series of different digs and landladies – the former hopefully warm and the latter kind – and theatres where it mattered what the dressing room was like and who you shared it with!

We performed at the Winter Garden Theatre in Drury Lane – which seemed a bit of a comedown after our previous appearance at the Haymarket with bombs falling all around.

I was staying with Yoma Sassburg and her husband Clifton Parker in St John's Wood at that time and was introduced to Andrew Burton, a portrait painter specialising in theatrical people, including Yoma. He painted a very good large painting of me. We have many other fine paintings of his around our barn, including one of Jack making up in a theatre. In later years he designed a poster for Emerson & Jayne. His paintings have been hung several times at the Royal Academy.

At last we set across the Atlantic again, this time with no fear of torpedoes. Our cast was very changed. We had some different dancers, two new pianists, and new stage staff. Even the firm that booked us was different; this time it was the Wagner Corporation rather than Columbia Concerts.

Most of the tour we travelled in large, quite comfortable buses which avoided the trouble of loading heavy baggage into taxis for distribution in hotels and theatres, a job Jack had not cherished on the previous tour, although he was extremely clever at beating greedy drivers' prices down.

We started the tour at the City Centre Theatre in New York. We now had formidable competition from other ballet companies such as the New York City Ballet and the Russian Ballet. They had so many more experienced and better dancers than we did, and the New York dance critic John Martin was not so enthusiastic about us. Rightly so, as we had so many newcomers in the company fresh from the Cambridge school, and unaccustomed to the Jooss style of interpretation – though Martin still praised *Green Table* as highly as before. We sensed that, as a consequence, the Wagner Corporation would not book us the lengthy provincial tour we had hoped for.

However, in the meantime, we were earning dollars and the shops were crammed with luxurious things, the like of which we in war-torn England and Europe had almost forgotten existed. And they were not rationed! We sent gifts of nylon stockings, slips, lovely pyrex coffee pots *etc* home and brought many luxuries back with us on our return.

After visiting Canada, we returned to a very cold English winter in Cambridge before setting forth again for the continent, visiting Holland, Denmark, Switzerland and Paris once more.

By the time we reached Paris the weather was quite warm and when

JOOSS BALLET

THE CONTEMPORARY DANCE – THEATRE

Artistic Director: KURT JOOSS

In Association With

THE ARTS COUNCIL OF GREAT BRITAIN

Exclusive Repertory:

"PANDORA"
Symbolic Ballet

"COMPANY of the MANOR"
A Victorian Miniature

"SAILOR'S FANCY"
A Farce

"LE BOSQUET"
Eighteenth Century Idyll

"THE GREEN TABLE"
Dance-Drama

"A BALL IN OLD VIENNA"
Vienna—1840

"BALLADE"
After an Old French Chanson

"THE PRODIGAL SON"
Dance Legend

"THE HEROES"
Comic Ballet

"PAVANE"
To the Memory of an Infanta

"THE BIG CITY"
Impressions of Metropolis

"A SPRING TALE"
Romantic Ballet

FIFTEENTH SEASON   SIXTH AMERICAN TOUR

JOOSS BALLET GENERAL MANAGER — Gabor Cosso

TOUR DIRECTION

CHARLES L. WAGNER, Manager   EDWARD W. SNOWDON, Associate Manager
511 Fifth Avenue, New York 17, N.Y.

AUTHORIZED AGENT FOR AMERICA Leon Greanin — 33 WEST 46 STREET, New York 19, N.Y.

not busy dancing evenings at the Theatre des Champs Elysées, we would visit the Louvre or go up the Seine to Bougival, the department stores. In August 1947, after another English tour, the Ballets Jooss as it then was closed down, as Jooss had decided to return to Germany and reform. The poster of the Theatre Royal, Newcastle, hangs on our kitchen wall and states: 'The cast will include Noelle de Mosa, Ulla Soederbaum, Joy Bolton-Carter, Hans Zullig, Rolf Alexander, Jack Skinner.'

Autumn 1947

Jack and Nigel Burke strolled through the sunny Cornish lanes that autumn singing 'Oh what a beautiful morning, Oh what a wonderful day!' We had come down to Cargreen before the two of them joined the cast of *Oklahoma!* at Drury Lane.

At the time Jack and I had no home of our own and, after a breath of Cornwall, spent the time with our relations until we were able to rent rooms on the top floor of a large house not far from Blackheath station. From there, we could reach London easily and quickly, Jack for a lengthy period in the cast of *Oklahoma!* and me for a regular dose of ballet classes. I joined the Dancers of London at a West Street studio where Vera Volkova taught, and we crowded into a tiny changing room with the likes of Margot Fonteyn and Moira Shearer. I also attended Goncharov's 'double work' classes in a studio below, and classes with Anna. I enjoyed this period of improving my technique, though I never achieved that classical dancer's figure Mme de Valois required.

It seemed at the time classical dancers were eager to acquire a modern technique, and vice versa. Jack, although he did not consider it a pleasure as I did, also took solo classes for a time with Espinosa. He must have felt he had to live up to the standards of the ballet boys who were constantly practising turns in the wings. With his strong harmonious physique he would have made a virtuoso ballet dancer, had he started his career in a classical school.

I now had another job; six dancers were needed to perform a short sketch in *Carissima!* each being a different character. Having been picked out in Volkova's class as a suitable urchin, I joined that company, leaving Jack at home for a while. Dressed in rags, and hurtling round the stage in the sketch we had to perform, I had the pleasure of reading a very complimentary line about myself in a Birmingham paper. It had been a long time since I had lapped up any flattery for a performance which would have been for a part in *Green Table*. My ego suffered a sad blow, however, when Agnes de Mille came over to put on *Carousel* and I travelled up to London to audition for the main dancing part. I had even been practising my American accent on phrases such as 'Ar hait yoo!' I didn't stand a chance as Sally Gilmour, leading dancer from the Ballet Rambert, coveted the same part and rightly got it. Agnes, whom I had not met since the New York days, was kind enough to congratulate me on my dancer's progress since that time.

On the telephone, Jack told me from Cornwall where he and his parents had been staying, that his mother had died of cancer. She was seventy eight, had suffered a fall down the steps of an old-fashioned tram on the Old Kent Road and had been somewhat depressed at having to

DAVIS
THEATRE
CROYDON

Licensee and Managing Director
ALFRED DAVIS

EMILE
LITTLER'S

ANNIE GET
YOUR GUN

Music
and Lyrics by
IRVING BERLIN

Book by HERBERT & DOROTHY FIELDS

THE RODGERS & HAMMERSTEIN
NEW YORK MUSICAL SUCCESS PRESENTED
BY ARRANGEMENT WITH
CHAPPELL & CO. LTD.

PROGRAMME - - - SIXPENCE

Jack as the Indian Chief Wild Horse in Annie Get Your Gun

move out of a very nice flat in Harrow.

Jack's father was a wonderful man of very high principles, and had been long a member of the Peace Pledge Union, as well as Editor of *Peace News*. He lived later in the house of a friend who took over the editorship after his retirement, until Jack was able to buy him a nice little flat on Muswell Hill. Soon after, Jack and I danced in the 1951 Glyndebourne Season, as Sigurd Leeder was doing the choreography for *Idomineo, Marriage of Figaro, Don Giovanni* and *Fuerza del Destino*. To arrive in time for rehearsal each day we had to arise at an unearthly hour to catch a train to Lewes from London, but that season was a pleasant experience in such congenial surroundings and later we took lodgings nearer to Glyndebourne.

I laugh now when I recall Fritz Busch's loud expostulation as he stopped the orchestra during Jack's leap as a Roman soldier down centre stage at the dress rehearsal of *Idomineo*: 'Who ees thees chumping monkey?' Choreographed by Sigurd Leeder, the monkey went on jumping until the end of the season!

Jack had spent almost two years in *Oklahoma!* It became a tedious grind for him after a while, and it was a relief when he was able to tour as the leading dancer in *Annie Get Your Gun*, making a most spectacular Red Indian Chief. As the understudy of the dancing 'Curly', Nigel Burke remained longer in *Oklahoma!*, before joining the revue *Oranges & Lemons* partnering Ulla Soederbaum from the Ballets Jooss. The boredom of the Drury Lane days was as usual alleviated, as it was in the Addenbrooke's Hospital period, by the continuation of Jack's bagmaking hobby in the dressing room, the products of which augmented our meagre finances once again.

The chorus dressing rooms at Drury Lane Theatre were up uncarpeted stone stairs, the dancers being on the top floor. The singers on the floor below depended on the clatter of dancers' cowboy boots descending as a cue for their next combined entrance. One night, Jack, on whom all depended, with his nose deep in a handbag, forgot to give the signal. There was poor old Ali Hakim the pedlar, at the end of his lines, pacing up and down the stage, waiting to be relieved by the crowd! Bad mark Jack – he'd nearly brought the curtain down on Ali Hakim!

While Jack was in either *Oklahoma!* or *Annie Get Your Gun*, I decided I must take a job, however menial, in order to give him a rest and be the one to earn our keep for a while. This I did by joining *Humpty Dumpty*, the Christmas pantomime at the Palladium, choreographed by Pauline Grant. The stars were Norman Evans as the dame, Noelle Gordon as principal boy and Peggy Mount as some sort of a witch – although a witch in *Humpty Dumpty* seems rather odd! The other male principal was Terry-Thomas who did a spot at the end that seemed equally out of context in *Humpty Dumpty*. Nigel Burke, recently with Jack in *Oklahoma!*, was to be the principal dancer, partnering Gillian Lynne, now famous for her choreography of the musical *Cats* and other long-running shows, while I tottered around in the chorus on my toes. Happening to be in the front line of some numbers, I was able to keep my chin up by being told that I 'stood out from the other dancers'! I associate that time with hearing one day that King George VI had died and I still see the shape of the buildings in the street as I walked along from the Palladium that day, ruminating on the drastic news.

In 1953 I became ballet mistress for *Paint your Wagon* at Her Majesty's theatre, and stayed the night secreted in my dressing room to witness the new Queen riding in her golden carriage on her way to be crowned. The next day I had a wonderful view from the roof of the theatre as she rode up the Haymarket.

As one who had not had responsibility for such a large cast of dancers before – and certainly never singers – I found this show quite a strain for it demanded experience and a certain amount of authority. Some of the singers strongly resented taking directions from a dancer, but it was always necessary for the ballet mistress to be in charge in musicals where so much colour and movement was expected in crowd scenes, when singers had to move around amongst dancers.

In spite of ideas for our own independent futures, Nigel, Jack and I all joined what was to be known as the New Ballet Company. The father of a Dutch dancer, Anija Wynberg, who had been a pupil with Jooss, put up the money to finance it. Anija and her pianist husband, Pat Harvey, brought in well-known choreographers to make the ballets, including Frank Staff, Walter Gore and Sigurd Leeder. All went well until promoters insisted that they should have an orchestra rather than a two-piano accompaniment for, sadly, finances would not run to it.

It was a pity, as Gore's ballet *Street Games* was very piquant and there was life in the company which I saw performing at the Wimbledon Theatre later when I had taken up the *Paint Your Wagon* job.

It was sad for the very good dancers of the New Ballet Company to be now out of work, but Margaret Booker, a very good dancer, teamed up with Nigel Burke. They worked on their own dance act, as Jack and I were intent on doing, and later became man and wife.

Shows in the 1950s

In between engagements Jack and I were sowing the seeds of an independent working life. We had joined the group of dancers, four men and four women, picked by Remi Martell who had come over from the States to choreograph a show at the London Casino, starring Jewel & Warriss. Performing a front-cloth spot was a young man called Peter Sellars, followed by a Spanish dance duo. Jack, an old hand at choreography from his Margaret Morris days, had impressed Remi with his audition dance composed to Stan Kenton's *Somnambulism*, and Remi chose Jack and me as two of his dancers. On Remi's arrival in England to start rehearsals, he found that the management had also held auditions and chosen other dancers! However, Remi refused to work unless with those dancers he had already picked.

The choreography of the strongest number we danced in the Casino show *Excitement* was – to say the least – as Kurt Jooss, after seeing the show, pronounced it – 'interesting'.

We ladies wore satin striped pants with plain white tops, the men in more or less unspectacular butch attire. The curtain rose on us all stationary and smoking du Maurier cigarettes in a blasé way – they were issued free to the show and were advertised on the programmes. Of course we dancers kept a supply of 'Willy Woodbines' in the dressing room, as who in their right mind would stub out a good cigarette after only one pull at it, as we were required to do in that opening? Jack never was a smoker in real life, however, and I indulged in no more than one or two a day, but there were plenty of grateful folk for those du Mauriers that never hit the boards – and there was then no thought of smoking causing lung cancer.

Our Jooss days had made us lazy as far as creative activity in the war years. But, as a result of being in this show, we realised that we too could, with a little effort, sell our own dance wares to earn a living rather than relying on future musical show imports for employment. First, though, we would have to find an agent to link us up to the places we would hope to perform in.

In the early '50s we were in our mid-thirties, a mature age for a dancer though we comforted ourselves with a dictum of Kurt Jooss who considered a dancer was not interesting as a performer until he or she reached this ripe age.

Our independent career as a dance act was ahead of us, though we knew that we must still work for others in order to survive – often separately, which was something of a hindrance. When unemployed, Nigel Burke and I would attend very good free modern classes with David Lober who was at that time appearing in the show *Touch and Go* atthe Princes Theatre. At the same time Jack and I were composing solos and duets, helped often by George Erskine Jones and Johnny Heawood who was soon to choreograph the dances for *The Boy Friend* opening at the Players' Club.

It was not till the advent of *Excitement* at the Casino that Jack and I were able to work together. Margaret Morris had moved her school to Glasgow in order to be with her Scottish painter and partner J D Ferguson and she invited Jack to compose two ballets for her students. According to Jack's letters, he was having great difficulty working with a rather poor standard of trainees and was not very enthusiastic at Margaret's suggestion that we should share a programme with them at the Arts Theatre.

However, Margaret herself, having a name almost as renowned as Ruth St Denis, was later invited with her Celtic Ballet – licked into shape by Jack Skinner – to Ted Shawn's *Massachusettes*, known as *Jacob's Pillow* (or rather wickedly *as Pat's Mattress*, one of our well-known dancers, named Anton, having spent a season there!)

It was hard work rehearsing for that summer adventure of 1954, though we were able to work with more competent Scottish dancers willing to be drawn back into the fold, such as Scottish Bruce McLure who was often in Glasgow's *Five Past Eight Show*. Jack and I both danced in the company performing our own duets and appearing in the ballets which were strictly Scottish of course. Jack had made a complete ballet appropriately called *Glasgow Green*, which went down well though we were never entirely happy with the music.

In one tableau the group danced the famous *Road to the Isles* lilt, twirling scarves around, Margaret in their midst. Fortunately, Jack and I did not have to participate as we were changing in our dressing room for our Balinese candle number in which we were very adept at turning somersaults whilst keeping candles alight in both hands! We also danced a blues and boogie in between the Celts ballet number, after which I heard a male dancer had been extremely shocked at such a commercial touch, when I tore off the blues skirt to start the boogie in the leotard I had under it. Perhaps that's where Bucks Fizz got the idea for the choreography for their Eurovision Song Contest entry *Making Your Mind Up* in 1981.

We were entertained by our Dartington friend and well known notation scholar Ann Hutchinson, who had a cottage near by and later

Jack in Glasgow Green

married Ivor Guest, the dance historian and writer. We made many other good friends besides.

Independence 1953

Our first independent date was in the large Dorchester Restaurant, where diners ate and watched us being Red Indians to the music of one of our Oriental numbers. We had a five-piece band to accompany us and as was usual we paid 10% commission to an agent called Karl Hyson. He later booked us to do a month at the Churchill Club; we considered this to be as respectable as the Dorchester – until we saw the artistes' changing room. This turned out to be down a flight of stone steps in a dingy basement below the small square stage. Fortunately, the novelty of it all overrode the discomfort, and we had a friendly companion changing with us named Danny who was partnering Ted Gatty, a large comic transvestite. Danny, whose gift of a pretty ring at our parting I still treasure, was later to emerge as Danny La Rue.

We asked the electrician to light one of our dances with ultraviolet, which gave certain of our costumes, especially in the candle number, a rich coloured glow. We soon learned that this had been a mistake as many patrons who were unfortunate enough to have plastic teeth, and who were sitting near the beam of these lights, were rendered toothless when they smiled and complained to the manager! Needless to say, we were not invited back to the Churchill Club!

We were now an Act called 'Emerson & Jayne – Dancing With a Difference' with a brochure showing pictures of the several dances we had to offer. It was Sonny Zahl from the Foster Agency who considered that 'Emerson & Jayne' gave us more dignity than 'Jack & Joy', though I strongly objected to being expected to live up to the image of the then popular Jayne Mansfield – or any other sexy Jayne.

The reputable Foster Agency procured us many good dates, but unfortunately not through poor Sonny who, shortly after naming us, was killed when he fell over his balcony.

As I was starting on a new career, I was advised by Johnny Heawood, choreographer for *The Boy Friend*, to go and receive instruction in a good make-up for the Act by the noted Stanley Hall. Although I had all my teeth I did this, and learned on receiving false eyelashes that Mae West often slept in hers; also that Edith Evans had one crooked eye. I wonder how he knew about the eyelashes?

We were very grateful to the director Danny O'Neill for allowing us to use his large stage for showing our Act to various London agents. Our offerings were never longer than the duration of a gramophone record, and we were most surprised when the agent Roberto Gerard told us that if he was to sell an attraction it was usual for it to last ten or twelve minutes. We followed his advice by stringing several individual orientally-themed dances together into one complete number.

We then auditioned to managements who put on pantomimes and were surprised to be told that it was possible, once engaged, to do several seasons of the same production!

We – artistic little snobs – were horrified at the idea of such repetition. Little did we know how welcome a long-running pantomime would become in the future, and repeatedly! We were also told that in panto we would have to fight for that ten minutes of exposure we had to provide for most cabaret dates, as there would be far too many stars demanding time in the show.

We have to thank *Paint Your Wagon*'s pianist Norman and trumpeter Dick Barrell for orchestrating the music we used, for what we called our *Oriental Phantasy* before the Magic Carpet made its début. The music

Emerson & Jayne in pre-Carpet days

started off with Dick's rendering of *Big Noise from Winnetka*, moving into Norman's oriental composition for our candle dance, then Dick's rhythmic music for a fan dance, and into a pepped up version of *Winnetka* for the long streamers and flags to finish.

Emerson & Jayne established

After our return from *Jacob's Pillow*, we moved my parents from their solidly-built red brick house to a smaller countrified one further out of Leicester. Leicester was creeping up gradually to the original house; it had been so beautifully built, with carved and polished woodwork everywhere and a view over to the gates of Victoria Park – a view so wasted on those cars that were to stand in the showrooms that had been our dining and sitting room, for the house was bought by a Rolls-Royce dealer!

We were able to settle furniture and belongings into the same sorts of

positions as they had been in the old house, and the move proved not too painful to all concerned.

We then had a choice: to appear in a new London production to be produced by Robert Nesbitt, presumably in the same group capacity as at the Casino, or to join a tour of Northern cities in a show put on by a Mr Blackie who was trying out a promising young comedian called Jimmy Paige. We chose the latter, as we wanted to go ahead as Emerson & Jayne.

So off we set with costumes and props in our little Ford Anglia to join the cast of *Girls How Dare You* touring weekly the number 'Threes' 'Twos' or 'Ones' as the theatres were called by artistes. There would, of course, often only be a 'One' in smaller towns. When we wrote to parents, we never wrote the show's title on the notepaper. Not that my father would have been in any way shocked, as he had visited the Leicester Opera House to see the Ballets Jooss and was, I guess, quietly pleased with his daughter's dancing of the Young Girl in *Green Table* – though he had at the same time criticised a mistake in the skeleton design on Death's costume!

He had also admired Jack's Indian warrior when *Annie Get your Gun* visited the Opera House. After all, he had been a student in London in the Music Hall days and chuckled when he heard we would be doing a week at the Woolwich Empire, one of his old haunts.

It is said that to move one's habitat in old age shortens one's life span. Who knows? Father was eighty-four when he died and he had lived barely two years in the new house. Mama, thirteen years younger, was to live on in a place easy to run with the help of one trusted but aged servant.

After that tour with *Girls* and many more kindly landladies, we were offered a summer season on St Anne's Pier, our first experience of such a situation. We had a very good producer in Stanley Willis Croft who turned the varied elements of the concert party into a good little show. He later asked us to participate in the pantomime he was putting on in Folkestone, which we gladly accepted – the thought of Christmas by the sea was most attractive.

Folkestone 1955

Our first pantomime as Emerson & Jayne was *Robinson Crusoe*, held in the Pleasure Gardens Theatre, Folkestone, sadly no longer standing, seemingly now part of the large civic centre built on the site. The

outstanding actor was Ossie Noble ('The Clown Prince') who was playing the part of Man Friday. We would watch his classic deck-chair sketch with admiration – it fooled him every time he tried to unfold it to sit on. His endeavours were accompanied by grunts and suitable noises – obviously the language of his Island. We met Ossie and his wife many times on our travels, and became good friends.

We learnt that Ossie had been an orchestral drummer and indeed he incorporated this in his mime act, using the same 'goobledy' language.

Emerson & Jayne – An early nautical routine

This brilliant idea originated from the fact that both his parents had been deaf and dumb and must have sounded somewhat like Man Friday. Later, it prevented him from being hired for a good and almost permanent job in Paris that we were lucky enough to obtain, because the management thought it was a genuine vernacular and that the audience would never understand him! Admittedly, for this reason, they only engaged visual acts.

To the west of Folkestone and a little way off the sea front we found and stayed in an excellent vegetarian hotel which had once been the home of H G Wells. We were so comfortable and happy, and we strolled by the sea in warm sunshine on Christmas Day thinking how much better this would be than living in Blackheath.

We must have performed our oriental numbers in this pantomime as natives of Crusoe's Island. We certainly had no Flying Carpet at the time, as the programme features 'Eugene's Flying Ballet'. The local newspaper

wrote: 'Equally, if not more spectacular, is the dancing of Emerson & Jayne whose oriental fire dance is a polished and athletic feature.'

The electrician lit our brightly-coloured flags and streamers with fluorescent bars from above which enhanced their brilliance considerably, and from that time onwards we carried our own ultraviolet lamps with us. In following years we were very lucky in receiving pantomime contracts usually with oriental themes such as *Aladdin*, mostly for the Emile Littler management for whom Jack had worked as Wild Horse in *Annie Get Your Gun.*

Our act developed, and I was soon charming a great snake out of a large red basket which Jack, invisible in black, worked on its string from the back. Our first snake appeared in the summer in Colwyn Bay; he was called Samuel – I don't know why, but he received a first-night telegram in that name from a friend of ours! He was made painstakingly out of circles of paper strung together by cord and resembling the necklaces

Samuel Snake (and a Flying Carpet)

worn by Hawaiian dancers, enclosed in a painted cotton coat.

After the Music Hall, Variety

In gracing the boards of the Music Halls, we discovered that, as dancers, we were expected to open both halves. Fortunately Cissy Williams, that great lady at the head of Moss' Empires, recognised that we were both worthy of a better position on the programme and ruled that we were interesting enough to be placed as a Speciality Act in the second half. Alas, we were not able to entertain on these fine great stages for long because our public preferred to sit by the fireside and watch the TV.

To get good dates in the variety theatres it was essential to have an agent and luckily, as a result either of the very many good notices we had had, or of rumour, we managed to tour the Moss' Empires circuit in between panto and summer season, in shows such as Harold Fielding's *Music for the Millions* topped by George Formby.

We toured vast distances with this show. One summer Sunday, on the way from Newcastle to Torquay after packing ourselves, costumes, props and a tent into our little car we decided, after a few miles, weary after that week's exertions, to camp on the moors. We were soon soundly asleep in the midst of Mother Nature, waking up to a fine sunny day but feeling uncomfortably damp from below. We found that in the dark we had pitched our tent in a bog.

That week we stayed in fine digs where dark grey cliffs towered up at the back of the house. As in the previous summer at Bradwell outside Yarmouth, where we rented a charming little cottage, we invited parents and relations to stay with us and enjoy some sea air.

Leaving the theatre one night in Torquay, I was recognised by a member of the audience, who asked if I was not nervous of our snake? I didn't enlighten her as to its tameness. In fact, Sammy Snake tended to bruise himself too much on stage floors and was soon given a much more durable interior of soft rubber. He also acquired a wife and child – two children if one counts the wormlike creature that wriggled out of my flute and made for the basket to a military march on the drums!

The Margaret Morris Movement to which Jack Skinner owed his training, and which still attracts many students world wide, now has its headquarters in Scotland and is run by Jim Hastie, dancer and director, and Robin Anderson. In those days, and undoubtedly now, dancers learned not only to move, but every aspect of what goes into the presentation of a live show – costume designing and making, décor, lighting – the lot.

Jack, with his clever hands and vivid imagination, intelligence and humour, was therefore able to compose dances for us which truly lived up to the claim in our Emerson & Jayne brochure: 'Dancing with a Difference'. Luckily agents agreed, and we were kept busy in travelling shows, panto, variety, summer shows and cabaret, not to mention circus!

Television page

Our first experience of television took place at a Chelsea cinema. We were a dance accompaniment to a lady singer whose name I regret to say escapes my memory. Also on the bill was Terry Scott, whom we later met as lead in pantomime, and star of the show was Benny Hill.

The only thing I remember about that day was the absurd sight of a great big man and a small, rather ugly comedian playing a silly game of tennis. The little fellow turned out to be Charlie Drake whom we often saw on the TV screen hurling himself into dreadful predicaments; we wondered how he remained in one piece.

The next TV we did was something called *It's Up To You*. Here, a panel gave their opinions and criticisms of the acts presented to them. We received reasonable treatment – except from one lady judge on the subject of our costumes – which, as usual, Jack had made and which we considered suitably comic for the pantomimic oriental number we treated

Emerson & Jayne and the Boojums

them to. This lady judge thought our costumes should have been more glamorous and sparkling; sequins, jewels *etc*. Completely unsuitable for our humorous offering! Fortunately, the comments from the other members of the panel were most flattering.

And so was the verdict pronounced on us in a programme sent out from The Royal Hall, Harrogate, called *What Makes a Star* where we performed the prototype of our Oriental Act. This time the costumes, though scanty, were brilliantly sequined and jewelled as befitted the subject, and comedian Issy Bonn pronounced the most encouraging words: 'This Act will go far'.

There followed the most flattering fan mail from viewers and later work from Barney Colehan in charge of the Leeds City Variety programmes, both live and on television.

To earn respect – and a living in the variety halls – we had to become a 'Speciality Act' as it was called, which meant discarding all the short precious dances we had hitherto so conscientiously worked upon. Among these were *Nightmare* to Artie Shaw's clarinet solo; *Moon Honeymoon*, a rather acrobatic duet, in dark green painted tights to Stan Kenton's music; a rather good parody on his *Tango*, where Jack finished up on his back on the floor, pinned down by my pointed foot; a '20s number called *Corny Rag*; and a sentimental dance to Stan Kenton's *Interlude* breaking into a frenzied boogie.

Now, with Sammy Snake and family joining our company, the Oriental sections of *Going East* were strung together to be recognised as a worthy Speciality Act of at least ten minutes for billing in the second half of a programme. And so, until the sad demise of Music Hall – undoubtedly the fault of the coming of TV in people's homes – we found ourselves in shows topped by all the most famous light entertainers of the day.

On arriving at Chiswick Empire for the week, we found there was another Eastern-type act on the bill: Wilson, Keppel and Betty. Two rather elderly gentlemen befezzed and swathed in Arab clothes performed on a tray of sand, shuffling the most ridiculous steps in profile, were vamped by a luscious veiled young Betty. We learnt that this Betty was the daughter of the original (who had once been Jack Benny's partner in vaudeville) but the two gentlemen continued into old age. On our farewells at the end of the week, they complimented us, stating that we had 'a Classic Act'. When later we were used to this kind of environment, we realised what an extremely classic act *theirs* was! They would so often be imitated any time a touch of Eastern comedy was called for.

Our Christmas pantomime engagements had by now become fairly regular; the show often starred Jimmy Clitheroe ('the Clitheroe Kid') and

'Rubber Neck' Nat Jackley – who had the most amazingly comic walk, looking somewhat like a hiccup speeding across the stage.

We were to be with Jimmy in many pantos, though it must have been in a summer season in Blackpool when he proudly showed us his garden compost heap. I think of Jimmy, and the meticulous pride he took in his compost heap, every time I contemplate the neglected rotting one behind our barn.

I wonder how many different dames we have been associated with in panto? The first was Norman Evans in *Humpty Dumpty* at the Palladium and I have a feeling that Danny La Rue with his gorgeous wardrobe in Wimbledon last Christmas will be the last! Jack saw neither of these pantomimes as he was in *Oklahoma!* for the first and, though his Magic Carpet flew in Danny's at Wimbledon, Jack had already died.

We introduced the Magic Carpet into the Act at Hanley, where a stagehand was required to pull its base, a converted makeup box, by a rope, to exit stage right. He tugged with too much exuberance, exiting only the box and

Emerson & Jayne and two Magic Carpets

STRAND THEATRE

(By kind permission of SEND MANOR TRUST LTD.)

SUNDAY, 7th DECEMBER, 1958

at 8 p.m.

PROGRAMME

THE PUBLIC ARE INVITED TO BECOME MEMBERS OF THE
GREEN ROOM RAGS SOCIETY. ANNUAL SUBSCRIPTION
HALF A GUINEA. APPLICATION SHOULD BE MADE TO
HON. SEC., 8-9 ADAM STREET, W.C.2.

*The Object of the Society is "to augment the funds of the Green Room
Club Fund, which has for its object the provision of assistance to
those Members of the Fund who may be in need of temporary financial
help through illness or any other cause, also to give donations if agreed
to by the Committee to Theatrical Charities, and or create a fund
whereby these and or similar objects may be achieved".*

*Members of the Society only are permitted to buy seats for
the "Rags".*

leaving me on the Carpet, grounded and somewhat bruised! Our Stage Director was not pleased: 'TAKE IT OUT' he sharply ordered afterwards.

Jack, clever fellow that he was, was far from defeated. His next prototype was a small square contraption of wood and iron on four wheels and stood about two and a half feet off the ground. It was covered in black velvet, a finish which, we discovered, rendered objects more invisible than any other. Jack manipulated that trolley with a longish strut growing out of its back, with a hinge incorporated to allow it an up and down movement.

Before we started Carpet riding, however, we were invited to take part in a Green Room Rag at the Strand Theatre. This is a charity to benefit less-fortunate members of the theatrical profession, and we felt honoured to be included in the company of such artistes as Hermione Baddeley, Geoffrey Braun, Benny Hill, Henry Kendall, David and Anna Massey, Ron Moody, Paul Robeson, Cardew Robinson, Eleanor Summerfield, Naunton Wayne and many others.

There was also a ballet company a member of which nearly sabotaged our act by using our snake basket to take the weight off her feet, not realising that it was set ready for our quick stage entrance. The snake family would never have managed to make an entrance, so completely had her posterior tangled its threads and magnets. Fortunately, Jack arrived just in time to save the day, though the usual first-night type nerves were augmented with shock. From the wings as we took our curtain call, I heard Peggy Ashcroft exclaim: 'Follow That!' which restored our spirits considerably!

In 1960, we performed at another Rag, this time at the Adelphi; by then we were flying our Carpet. Johnny Hewer, Amanda Barrie, Fred Clarke and Roy Castle were among the cast. The press gave us a most complimentary notice:

> The second half had more pace. Emerson & Jayne did not give us a trick or appearance too many in their half evocation of Oriental Magic. In that respect, a pair of conjurers.

Moscow State Circus

That same year we received an offer to appear at Wembley in the Moscow State Circus. It was then an Equity ruling that certain visiting foreign companies must now include some English acts in their midst.

We were to open the second half as a sort of fanfare of mixed skills. There were some acrobats, a ballet dancer, a ballet and us, marching round the ring.

We were not to be allowed in the ring, as the Russians did not want us

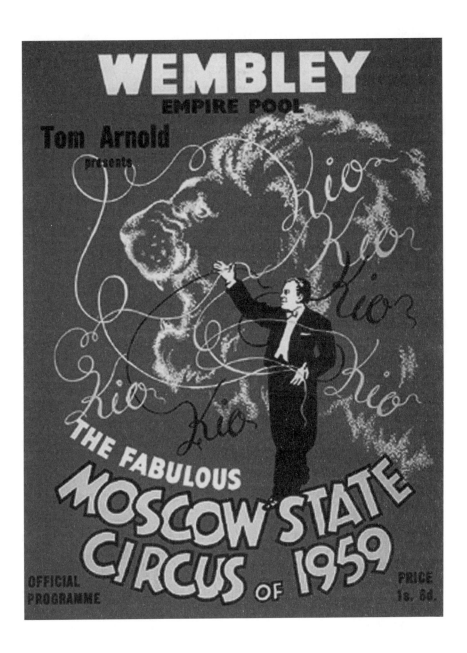

to pass over the secret traps down which they and their lions *etc* had to disappear mysteriously, and reappear from even more mysteriously.

Somehow or other, Jack and I did gain permission to traverse the whole of the inner ring, as we could not otherwise present our Act, which entailed a tour of the space, and flying gigantic streamers and a flag, under which Jack ran with me perched aloft on his shoulders.

For the finale, Jack led the Russians back into the ring, carrying an enormous flag, this time with hammer and sickle embroidered upon it. At the same time, hundreds of pigeons were released over the heads of the audience; Jack often recalled the sensation their wings created as they passed over his head, back through the tunnel. Later on we were to fly our big Carpet at another circus in Holland, where we performed our whole Act and they went to the trouble of laying a special floor over the sandy ring for us. They also draped black curtains around while an aerial act was engrossing the audience in the roof of the building.

During the period we were taking part in the Russian Circus at Wembley, we bought two homes. One was a green Dormobile, our very first home on wheels. It was almost new, and we bought it at a slight reduction, as it had been used as a demonstration model.

The other home we bought was a small attached house in Brockley, because the house in which we had a flat was to be sold. We tried to buy it but the family refused to sell to us; we suspected that they did not favour theatrical buyers!

However, the little house we bought was nearer to London and had been excellently cared for by the previous owners. We were delighted to discover a beautifully tiled bathroom off the small kitchen. The only drawback was the family of eleven children living next door, but they turned out to be well behaved on the whole – and we were often away on tour.

At Christmas we were off to do panto in Manchester, and the next year a Torquay summer season with Ken Dodd. That summer we took our collapsible 'Prout' dinghy with us and moored it at Babbacombe, camping nearby in our beautiful new Dormobile. When the sea was smooth and the day sunny, we would have idyllic sails around the bays.

After this pleasant summer, we were off to Iceland. We had to perform on an open floor, so we didn't take the Carpet with us that time.
I remember dancing Stan Kenton's *Interlude* and parts of our Oriental; then being entertained by an appreciative fisherman after our efforts, and the walk home to our Danish landlady's lodgings afterwards gazing at the

midnight sun and breathing in the all-pervading smells of sulphur – also present whenever one turned a tap on to wash oneself!

About this time, we met Don Saunders the musical clown and his wife at Bognor. Don kindly recommended us to his Paris agent, which led to many of our dates in France and elsewhere abroad.

Paris

So in the early '60s we found ourselves, props and costumes on the ferry bound for France. We were off to sell our very own show on the Continent. Without a partner as confident and dependable as Jack, I would have been terrified of such an adventure! The very thought of driving into the busy Paris traffic was awesome. We knew our night club was just off the Champs Elysées but made first for the Quais on the banks of the Seine, parking not far from the Eiffel Tower, where we slept the night. We spent two or three days on this admirable site without disturbance, and we often parked there on future visits to Paris. However, our usual home for the van and ourselves was beside the Seine in the Bois de Boulogne, where many other artistes working in Paris camped. *Holiday on Ice* caravans were often our neighbours, and we became quite friendly with other performers whom we met again on later visits. I believe tourists were supposed to stay no more than a month, but Madame was always very welcoming to artistes, whom she appeared to regard as a cut above the tourists, and she turned a blind eye if we needed to stay a few extra days. In summer, the camp was not so attractive because of all the holidaymakers and we found it less easy to obtain our favoured site near the river and to connect to an electric socket – for which we gladly paid extra.

It was only a short walk from the camp to cross the bridge over the river to Suresnes to buy good food. We worked so often in Paris that this neighbourhood became almost a second home to us. On one occasion they were doing some street repairs and had torn the name from the boarding; we seized it and it is now fixed to the wall at home: 'Rue Etienne Dolet'; he was a French humanist and martyr.

Our first independent appearance on stage in Paris was to be at a night club in Rue Pierre Charron, recommended in a book by one of the Mitford sisters. It was called Le Sexy which name, although it may have earned the club its popularity, embarrassed us when notifying friends and relations of our whereabouts, and we grumbled to ourselves when our employers could hear us. On returning for a later engagement at Le Sexy, we found that we were now working at Le Milliardaire. Someone had taken the hint!

Admittedly the show was rather shocking because half the acts were extremely attractive near-nudes who almost performed the sex act in their dance presentations – which was quite a revelation to one who had not seen a nude show before. The headroom on stage was so low that we were unable to do our piquant entrance with palanquins and boojums, starting instead with an eccentric candle dance. As for the finale, I got a stiff neck sitting on Jack's shoulder and trying to avoid the low ceiling as I waved the coloured ribbons and streamers.

We appeared several times in a restaurant night club at the end of the woods called L'Orée du Bois. It seemed we were always there just before chestnut time, as I associate it with the beautiful heavy hanging blooms of white candles around it pressing against the windows of the artistes' lavatory. The stage conditions however were quite unsuitable and lethal for Jack's unseen exit with the Magic Carpet, as there were steps down to the wings.

The other Parisian venue we played several times was the restaurant on the first platform of the Eiffel Tower, where conditions were equally formidable. Jack often described the pleasant sensation of being clad in his invisible black cloak and under UV lights, able to see Paris spread all around him through the great windows, but unseen himself. He felt as if he was a ghost!

To reach the artistes' quarters backstage, one had to pass the kitchens, cooks' and waiters' departments. The waiters would make a collection of the patrons' unfinished wine bottles ready for their own consumption later, but as our performance was over before they could return to their treat, we were able to sneak a few nips from their hoard as a reward for our efforts.

The lavatories of this part of the tower were somehow slung in the iron supports which, according to Jack, were becoming very rusty! No wonder that shortly after that, we were told they had done away with the 'Diner Spectacle étage'.

The move to Stanford and the large Carpet

Returning on the boat at the end of a Paris engagement to our house in Brockley, we lit upon a newspaper advertisement for a bungalow, barn and field at Stanford in Kent. Always having admired converted barns, we went to view the property. The bungalow had not been long built and was in good condition. As the owner was leaving for Australia we decided to buy and turn the barn into our home later.

The father of all the children next door in Brockley helped us pack up our belongings and drove down with us to Stanford village to help at that end. We had only a few days to settle in before we had to leave for a panto at the Alexander Theatre in Birmingham. We were still only flying our

The Barn before conversion

little Carpet, but this proved effective enough for Derek Salberg, the manager of the theatre, to arrange for it to fly on a Blackpool Pier the following summer. Derek and Dick Condon, of Dublin Gaiety and later Norwich Theatre Royal, were among the nicest managers we ever met.

It was not until the following Christmas in a Sunderland panto that I rode a large colourful Carpet over the orchestra pit. I had to seat myself quickly, crosslegged, in the centre of the thing, as Jack lowered the front end of the apparatus to the ground. Strangely enough, I never felt nervous of being tipped over on to the drummer's head.

This large Carpet had developed a long way since the prototype we had auditioned without our proper lighting. At that time, if I wanted to fly higher from my starting pad, Jack had to press down on a kind of hinged lever behind my bottom, and for some reason the Carpet tipped me off backwards. I felt somewhat foolish after that experience.

South to Nice

We must have been seen in Paris at Le Sexy by the French representative of *Das Organ*, a little old Jewish fellow who took it into his head to become our manager, telling us about other successful acts he had launched, and how he would obtain an engagement for us in the Dortmund Wintergarten. We let him do this as we had no idea at the time what an international act should earn, and knew that Le Sexy should have been paying us more than a meagre FF70 nightly. However, we vegetarians, who seldom ate in restaurants or lived on the tiles, found we were able to save even on that amount. To performers applause is as good as money. Had we had a family as our friends at the Casino were deciding to have, we might have behaved differently.

We left Paris in the hot summer of 1962 as our agent had fixed us a date in Nice. It was exciting to be visiting the coastal resorts I had thought only sophisticated people went to, to escape our winter climate. Jack talked of the Summer Schools that the Margaret Morris Movement had held in Antibes, and showed me a picture Margaret had sent of Ferguson sunning himself on a rock with her.

It was good to leave the heat of Paris and we had time before our engagement started at Le Maxims to park our van almost on the seafront. I shall never forget the pleasure of the first sight of that azure sea as we rounded a bend. We soon immersed ourselves in it before moving on to the next bay for the night. It was high summer, and the camps were full of holidaymakers, but we always managed to find a quiet corner and fix our sunblinds and mosquito nets. The stage working space at Le Maxims was disappointing but, as we were still really a dance act, we gave them our Red Indian number to start with, bow and arrow tricks *etc*, then the oriental candle dance, with snake charming and streamers to follow. We spent our days basking on beaches.

On 15 July, I wrote to Mama:

> We are parked along the beach which, even out here at St Laurent, is very crowded today. We have found our own private one on a spit of No Man's Land beyond the Airport, where the Var river comes out between little islands. We more or less live in bathing costumes, the sun and the sea, because the coast has become the only bearable place in this heat, and we look like a pair of chestnuts.
>
> We have, however, made two delightful excursions into the foothills and visited two little fortress towns called Cagne and St Paul, full of narrow winding streets where many artists live. We looked into a house in St Paul where we knew an ex-MMer lived and painted. Her door into

a little cave-like room was open but we only encountered six or seven cats! and discovered she ran a small theatre at the back.

These two little citadels were built on pinnacle rocks like fairytale giant fortresses or castles with their ramparts intact just as they were in the 14th century . . .

We are thinking. now we are so near, of going into Italy, then back to look at Cannes and Antibes. We will also visit a Mr Marouani in Monte Carlo who may provide us with further work in this area.

Morocco August 1962

Mr Marouani fixed a contract for us far down in Marrakech and so we set off in the heat of summer in our motor caravan on the long journey through Spain to Africa. We chose to travel the flattest route as we had a slight petrol block still in spite of garage attention, and the mountain routes caused the poor engine to boil all too readily. We passed through a France quite new to us – Montpelier, Perpignan, Aix-en-Provence – on bumpy roads in scorching heat, camping in Brignolle and Arles on the way. We had time to admire the wonderful buildings dating back to Roman days; the great Arena in Arles looked as modern as Hitler's 1936 one in Berlin. In Brignolle we experienced the first cool night since we left England and clutched around after blankets. When we reached the frontier into Spain, we vowed never to travel on French roads in early August, the month in which the inhabitants spill out of their towns in holiday masses, searching for sun, sea and fresh air! It took us one-and-a-half-hours to get through the frontier into Spain, so strict was the customs check on French and Spanish nationals. They hardly glanced at our passports when we finally crawled up to the barriers.

The mountainous route seemed very primitive and we carried on to Barcelona before sleeping. The next day, we immersed ourselves in a cold sea on the Costa Brava. We had been told to call in on the theatrical agent Señor Cortes in Madrid, but unfortunately were too late for his office hours and had to be content with a French-speaking deputy. We guessed this would not result in employment in the near future, although we later returned to two very pleasant dates in Madrid's Florida Park.

We stopped next in Zaragossa, the town founded by Augustus Caesar where there was a wonderful 14th-century Baroque cathedral. We would have visited this, had not Jack been challenged by a gendarme who we feared was about to cart him off to the police station (as had happened to Lukas on the Jooss tour of South America) for wearing shorts. Luckily, he was barred only from entering the cathedral. Nowadays they've gone to the topless extremes as we have. Apart from this, it was pleasant travelling among the Spanish who, when our tea and coffee supplies ran out, were so much kinder to us than the French. They smiled, tried to understand us and be helpful, so that one forgave the bumps and ruts in their roads. History and proximity, I guess, make the French suspicious of us.

Thank heavens there was no mountain climbing out of Madrid for the poor van. Madrid is about 2,000 feet up. (The highest we have ever been was Peru and Bogotá. Peru was 16,000 feet; but that was in a communal bus hired by the ballet.)

There was then a 3,000-foot climb to Córdova on a well-graduated road and within 300 miles of the city we pulled off the road to spend the night.

We beheld the authentic Córdova the next morning – its Moorish flavour was similar to the South America we had visited during the war. Now we were able to visit the 8th-century cathedral, considered one of the oldest Moorish mosques in the world. We really felt as if we were in Arabia even as we crossed a fine old Roman bridge, intact, though originally also built by the Moors.

After driving through a very tropical Moorish Sevilla, we were off down to the Atlantic coast where a refreshing breeze blew over marshland, reminding us of the sand and mud of the Blakeney salt marshes. Here, though, were olive trees in addition, and as we were only thirty miles from Cadiz, and the tip of Spain, we decided to make camp after a meal of papayas. Then, after a scrambled-egg breakfast among the cactus, we set off for Gibraltar and the ferry.

We had been delighted to buy a bottle of sherry for five shillings in Jerez and hoped, now our English supplies were depleted, to be able to stock up in Gibraltar. We were successful, but apart from fuel everything – tea, oats, biscuits *etc* – was very dear as the goods were of necessity imported.

We had been able to feed in Spain most inexpensively. As we had to shop, and get the van serviced, and there was only one ferry sailing to Tangier each day, we spent the night in a camp high above glorious beaches, to which we descended for two swims in a rather cool sea, then inspected the Rock and the terrain around us. We noticed that the Atlantic breezes in the scorching sun sometimes clashed with the Mediterranean ones, bringing down a white misty cloud and with it a damp and oppressive atmosphere.

Tourists told us that the roads in Morocco would be better and the heat not so oppressive. Fedala, we learnt, was now the Moroccan name for Marrakech and our first impressions were of a long strip of beach, deserted except for two women fully clothed in rumpled national dress about to fight their way through high breakers for their daily bathe.

Behind all this was a sumptuous park of tropical growth in which stood the Casino where we were to perform and where we were allowed to park our van.

The star of the show was Victor Borge, but of our performance on the first night I can only write the word 'Disaster'! We left the theatre in shame with our tails between our legs. The electrician had failed to switch on our ultraviolet lights and, as a result, the whole Act was ruined.

Luckily, the next day we succeeded in convincing the management that they had got something rather special after all, because the head gardener was ordered to direct us to an idyllic and private part of the grounds.

International Magic

We were really starting a new phase in life now that we were middle aged, but I suppose it kept us young and vigorous. We were turning forty three and forty four, and were starting off for a cabaret date in Amsterdam. We didn't enjoy this experience, not being used to cramped conditions on a night club stage and the unfamiliarity of the commercial atmosphere. Being at this stage only 'Dance Impressionists' we were not yet carrying our ultraviolet lamps around; later, with our own equipment, we felt safe in our own milieu where we could not easily make out whether or not the audience was attentive.

It seems incredible now that we could receive a telegram from a Swiss agent and set off to Geneva's Grand Casino to perform for only three days at a salary of 500SF for the lot! But Switzerland was always alluring for its scenery of lakes, mountains, good roads and shops – not to mention good francs. We always felt unrushed and at peace there; perhaps for me it was a subconscious childhood memory of a boat trip on Lac Leman with Mama, when we visited my elder sister at her Lausanne finishing school.

But although now we could call ourselves an International Act, we definitely preferred to work nationally. We had completed the mechanism for a fine large Magic Carpet that had had its maiden flight at the Sunderland Empire and were congratulated by the very nice manager of the time.

From then on, each year we expected to be in a pantomime at Christmas in a nice large warm theatre in England, Ireland or Scotland. There are so few subjects where the hero or heroine does not get in to some sort of Oriental predicament, allowing Emerson & Jayne to work their magic.

Our Oriental dances, never in a serious vein, we had woven together into a programme lasting up to ten minutes, each section relating in some fashion to the next. This sequence became 'Emerson & Jayne and their Oriental Fantasy' or, as we performed mostly on pantomime boards, 'and their Magic Carpet'.

Very soon, to our surprise, we found that we had by accident – and Jack's ingenuity – joined the world of magicians, and from then on we were invited to perform at many English and foreign Conventions and Magic shows, and received many flattering notices.

Now, a show made up only of magicians – as we learnt in Geneva for the first time – can be a nerve-racking experience, for nearly all of them depend at least in part on their props for the success of their act, and these props have to be in the wings, immaculately set and ready for action pending a quick change of scene. One hopes that there will be a compère to make an announcement or spin a yarn in front of the curtain while one sets one's own paraphernalia. The first night can be a real ordeal, having to depend also upon the theatre staff for help in lighting, music and other cues – in fact, it usually took a week before things ran smoothly and we could enjoy working.

Music was often a problem too; it was heaven returning to those places with good orchestras who enjoyed playing our music and were able

Outside the Scala Theatre, 1964

to improvise extra effects to the quaint things that happened in the act. We found this at the Hansa-Theater in Hamburg and in several places in Paris. We had always to beware of One Nighters, and were most relaxed about our music when we could sign up for a long pantomime and summer season.

After the get-in and rehearsal, The Magic Circle Convention show we took part in at the Scala in London in October 1964 was a baptism into the world of magic. We felt most honoured to be admired as magicians with a good position on the programme. As a result of this we made many good friends among magicians and were asked to take part in several further shows in other countries. Jack's gift for inventiveness and imagination, and the training in art and dance we had both had, resulted in an act entirely different from anyone else's. In addition to magical effects, we were now working almost entirely in 'black' (ultraviolet) light, which gave colour and brightness to cheer a show – although for just two of us it was rather ambitious and exhausting.

Summer 1964

After we got back from the Geneva Casino, our agent Johnny Riscoe fixed us a pleasant two-month season in a theatre on the seafront at Rhyll. Arthur Askey topped the bill with feed Jerry Desmond. We stayed a little inland in the grounds of a house belonging to a charming elderly lady. By now we were earning a three-figure salary as befitted a respectable Speciality Act – the mighty sum of £125 weekly, the like of which we had never earned before in England.

On one occasion, we agreed to do two Sunday shows at the local Butlin's Camp; for forfeiting our Sunday rest we were to receive £50. We had often wondered what a Butlin's was like, so much advertised at the time, but not quite our idea of holiday bliss!

We performed that weekend on a very large stage to a very large and enthusiastic audience, and had nourishment among them in a large canteen. It all seemed very pleasantly set out in spacious surroundings and perfect for children.

At the back of our lady's home where we were living in our Dormobile was a pen where her black poodles lived, and during our stay they gave birth to the most delightful puppies. These had grown somewhat by the end of our season and we could not resist buying one; we acquired the bitch and our stage manager, seeing her in our dressing room, was so enamoured of her that he set off and bought her slightly larger brother. We called ours Midge and she accompanied us to all future engagements, often smuggled past the stagedoor man in a shopping bag.

We had become acquainted with Johnny Heawood through friends who had worked with him in London reviews such as *Oranges and Lemons* and *Twopence Coloured*. He was a member of the Players Club, later choreographing the dances for *The Boy Friend* Sandy Wilson was to write and put on there before its transfer to many other large theatres.

We would visit the Players as Johnny's guests, when Don Gemmell would be sitting as chairman in his kilt and running the theatre with Reginald Woolley, who employed us that September into October. What a delight it was to witness Hattie Jacques' wicked twinkle as she exited stage left after her piquant naughty song, and all those other good artistes including Joan Sterndale Bennet, Maurice Browning, Clive Dunn, John Hewer and Vida Hope.

It was rather difficult squeezing our large Carpet into the very narrow stage at the Players. Fortunately, with Jack's skill and effort, there was enough depth to manoeuvre it and we were able to fly off through the middle of the black curtains at the back. Peter Greenwell gave us very nice piano accompaniment as we had no taped music at that time. On later engagements under the Arches, we were sensible enough to fly the small cabaret Carpet, though this vehicle could not achieve the spectacular trip over the footlights.

We received marvellous applause from the Players audience, almost as heart warming as that we'd experienced from an audience of magic-minded folk!

Mr Fred Thorpe

We introduced Midge the poodle pup to Mama after we got back from our summer season in Rhyll. The Carters had always kept dogs, though they were usually cocker spaniels. We had no qualms therefore in leaving Midge in Leicester when we set off to Paris for another spell at Le Sexy. By now, Mama's legs didn't like walking too far beyond the garden but our faithful Thorpe delighted in taking Midge for her daily exercise.

Fred Thorpe came into the family as a result of one of the many afternoon bridge sessions my mother took part in. He belonged to one of the players and was the only male servant amongst several females, who resented his presence among them. When the lady regretfully sighed that she would have to give him notice or lose her maids, Mama offered to take him on and, though he was sometimes a great trial to her, he was a good worker and extremely kind, and faithful, possessing just a little more brain power than Midge – to whom he was devoted. He had bought himself a smart moped to reach the town for shopping but this entailed a driving test which proved an embarrassing experience. He failed it four times because he could never answer the questions put to him. Mama had to write a little note to the examiner finally, explaining his nervous character or some such! I think he was devoted to us as well for, after Mama's death, we took him to live with us in Kent, where he kept house for us when we were away on our foreign travels until, as he aged, we managed to set him up in a very nice room with his own kitchen in an Age Concern Settlement.

He wept in anguish at this move but soon started to enjoy the friendly environment there. It was not far along the country lanes from us and I would take him shopping every Thursday, bringing him home to tea with us afterwards.

Alas, he died the very day we had left to start a month at the Hansa-Theatre; fortunately, our nephew Timothy was able to arrange his funeral.

Switzerland

We never actually enjoyed the working hours of our foreign travels, and we often had to drive through night to our next venue. The stages of Good old England were by far the best to manoeuvre our props on, with perhaps the exception of one in Zurich next to the Opera House, where we took part in several magic seasons before touring with the show in proper theatres and casinos. However, it was worth the suffering – after all, we were being paid to visit the countries most other people would have to pay a lot of money to visit. The important thing was to keep healthy and strong enough for both work and pleasure.

When we were in places such as Geneva and Lausanne out of the holiday season, we had the caravan and the camp almost to ourselves. The Geneva camp was near Vesenaz, on the other side of the Lac, and we would often cycle into Geneva when fine.

One Sunday we set off in the little van in the direction of the distant Jura one could see beyond the town, and up to Creuzet Fierny where there were ski lifts to the top. We decided it was too cloudy to drive the van higher, so we continued on foot up the green slope of the mountain until we were treading through snow. The top seemed in reach by now and, like fools, we decided to continue. Soon we were 4,000 feet up; the snow was up to our thighs, my wellingtons were full of snow and Jack fought to keep his galoshes on his feet.

But, Hooray! There was a cosy ski hotel at the summit where we recovered on glasses of brandy; after we were warm again, we descended by ski lift. They say dancers are masochists; so also must polar explorers and Everest climbers be! We had to laugh when we looked up the mountain from below – the slope seemed almost vertical. How stiff we felt after that little adventure.

The Hansa-Theater

After Geneva, we took it in turns to drive the seven hundred miles to
Hamburg with a five-hour break on the first car park of the German
Autobahn. Before that the van had started to sway and we lost two hours
getting a puncture attended to. I must say the German police were very
kind and helped us get enough air into the spare tyre to get us to a garage.
Hamburg seemed very cold at six in the morning; people were going to
work while we searched around for the Hansa-Theater.

The British had dropped bombs on it during the war; it was a good
target situated very near the Hauptbahnhof. Nothing of it had been rebuilt,
and the space it once stood in was now a large theatre car park on which
artistes were allowed to live in their caravans, and which provided shelter
for performing animals. We were to live on this park during many further
visits to the Hansa, but for this month we rented lodgings in a large house
next door. It obviously belonged to the new Theater which was now
smaller and fitted in along the left stone wall of the original. We were
given an enormous high-ceilinged room in a flat belonging to two elderly
kind squat landladies, and had use of their kitchen and bathroom as
seemed customary – and all for a very reasonable rent. Mind you, the
Hansa never paid large salaries and never engaged artistes through an
agent, preferring to make the bookings themselves after travelling to see
a performance. On future visits Jack managed to squeeze a few more
DMarks though, like most artistes, we were not performing just for money
but also for enjoyment and approval, hoping always for suitable
conditions in which to achieve these.

The first night at the Hansa would nearly always go without a hitch,
thanks to an organised and professional staff, civilised conditions and
reliable orchestra, especially after it became used to our music. In later
years, the over-important conductor was replaced by a very sensitive and
talented Polish pianist who improvised on a synthesising type of organ.
We were delighted at the accompaniment he created for our puppet
animals and strange happenings.

Our act always received respectful attention. Most of the acts kept
coming back; Ossie Noble, who was Man Friday in our first panto and an
excellent comedian, said: 'It's much better than the Palladium for me'. We
had a nice dressing room and use of a shower, and there was always coffee
in the Green Room. The audience sat at shelflike little tables in front of
the rows, served by maids in white frilly aprons and caps; it was as if the
clients were in church behind their decorated brass pews.

An entry in my diary reads: 'After Easter, I must go and visit my old
Wigman friend Ilse Klasen. Do you remember? She married the president
of the Deutsche Bank after the war; I met him then in London and sent

coffee back to Ilse.

'There is a troupe of performing poodles of all sizes living in the courtyard. I hope Midge is behaving. She would be just as clever at doing the tricks they perform on stage'.

We returned to the Hansa many times, living in our van in the big courtyard created by the war. It was a novelty being right next to the theatre and a stone's throw from our dressing room where we would spend most of the day – not that our motor caravan was uncomfortable. We had by now had a most elaborate and comfortable home custom built on a Leyland lorry with all mod cons. The only luxury we did not allow ourselves was a shower compartment but there was usually a shower in the theatres we visited. As we were not programmed to appear until the last part of the first half, and then again at the finale, there was no longer any need to hasten from distant lodgings.

The Hansa-Theater

The very first time we appeared at the Hansa we were definitely dancers rather than magicians, performing as we then did our Balinese-type dance with lighted candles. In later visits we had discarded this section as most theatres had by then very strict fire regulations – and in any case we had no wish to exert our aging selves overmuch, preferring to let the props such as comedy animals and situations entertain the audience. As a result, it became with time a much stronger act. Originally, it had been the candles, along with our sparkly costumes, that had given us our reputation for being very suitable as Christmas fare. After discarding the candles, we started the act with a six-armed Siva figure holding electric-type candles as a prelude to my charming the snakes from their basket – all, of course, before the latter started to misbehave.

Blackpool and Glasgow

> *Blackpool Evening Gazette*: 'The most entertaining act was the most novel Emerson & Jayne's Going East.'
>
> *Tit Bits*: '... and the prize novelty act of the season, Emerson & Jayne's magically lit Oriental Fantasy'.

After another month in Dortmund's Wintergarten, we returned to England to do a nice long summer season at the Queen's Theatre Blackpool. We did three seasons at the Queen's; the first time Tommy Cooper topped the bill; another time it was Jewel & Warriss.

At the end of our act, as we flew the Magic Carpet off stage left, Tommy Cooper suddenly appeared from stage right sitting on a pram-like contraption, a makeshift luggage trolley he had borrowed from a small boy outside the railway station. Tommy careered along the footlights, pulled from the other side by a stagehand who hadn't reckoned with the considerable stage rake. I had flown over the orchestra; Tommy nearly landed in it!

When Jewel & Warriss topped the bill, one of their gags was to appear in a large fish tank full of water. It was not very popular with those who followed their act, especially Emerson & Jayne. Jewel & Warris didn't get wet at all but somehow their tank leaked a little, causing the dancers to slip around and our Chinese streamers to become sodden and stick to the stage floor.

When we had performed on Blackpool Central Pier, there was very little space for us and the orchestra was almost on a platform beside us. In those days we only had the miniature flying Carpet we had introduced at the Birmingham Alexander Theatre. Later, we did a summer season on Blackpool South Pier with Mike Terry (a very large-sized kaftan-wearing piano virtuoso), Joe Belcher, and a group called Candlewick Green. Mike Terry played on two pianos alternately; Winifred Atwell had given him a white one, on which he played Honky Tonk, the then modern jazzy rave, I suppose! The Grumbleweeds were in their first professional show after winning an award in Opportunity Knocks.

Here conditions were very favourable. We would smuggle Midge on to the pier as we had to do two shows daily, but when I took her out for some air I had to be so careful that her little paws didn't get caught in the gaps in the pier boards.

At weekends we would motor into the Lake District and row our rubber dinghy to the middle of Coniston Water when the weather was sunny. Midge loved those trips but we nearly lost her overboard the first time we stopped the engine away from the shore. She knew that when that happened one disembarked, so she leapt joyfully over the stern. Thank heavens we were able to grab her tail before she vanished completely.

That summer season lasted till the end of October – unheard of now – then we moved on to Glasgow, where Jimmy Logan had taken over and was putting on a pantomime at the Metropole Theatre. It was a completely Scottish show entitled *Tangle of the Isles*: with the famous Scottish couple Gracie Clark and husband topping the bill. We gave a charity show there attended by Princess Margaret, who asked us how we were able to ride the Carpet up to the height of her box.

We remained in Glasgow until the end of March. How lucky we were in those days with such long seasons!

Copenhagen

We had neither an English summer season nor a pantomime, so we became gypsies again and set off for the Valencia Theatre in Copenhagen arranged for us by the agent Syd Fox. Amazingly enough, we arrived on the waterfront at the same time as our friend Ossie Noble and his wife.

They, like us, had only just landed and were making for the tourist camp, but were playing at a different venue.

We had a few days to enjoy our surroundings before we had to start work. I remembered very little from my last visit after the war with the Ballets Jooss; it wasn't summer but dark and damp and I had to miss a few shows when I tore a calf muscle. I also remem-bered a ride I took on a switchback railway in the Tivoli

Gardens, sitting next to our wardrobe mistress who screamed with terror on the high swoops!

Jack and I watched the Harlequinade in the Peacock Theatre; it was rather childish but, as it was a period production, that was excusable. We met the stage director, who was from Dartington and knew many of our old acquaintances of the dance world. We had drinks, then went to a not-very-good ballet performance – not the Danish Royal Ballet, as it was the summer recess. We also saw Jose Greco and Co whose dancers were excellent but he himself was past it, though he made up for this with his overflowing personality.

On Sunday we visited the old Theatre Museum of 1780 which I had previously marvelled at; it was really charming, not unlike our old Bristol Theatre and the Leeds City Varieties. One stands at the back of the opened-up stage gazing through the proscenium arch to the Royal Box at the other end of the theatre. We took photos and recorded the music that was playing.

Another day we took a boat and floated on a very calm sea. I even swam, though Jack was never an eager swimmer and remained on board. There was so much to do that we were usually exhausted by the time we arrived to entertain the audience at the Valencia!

Of course we went along the harbour to visit the Little Mermaid. She is rather old fashioned for these days; no wonder someone had it in for her and took her head off. She's got a spare head now, because, after they'd fitted a replacement, they recovered the original one!

Unfortunately the Valencia went bankrupt during our stay and the manager had disappeared by the end of the month. We were some of the first artistes to arrive at the office to be paid before leaving; we received our salary but heard later that not everyone else had.

The Colt Saloon, Lunel

Leaving Denmark to reach Lunel, we took a boat over to Germany. There was a 1,200 mile journey in front of us, but we had time as it was only to be a fortnight's stay at the Colt Saloon. The weather was still very hot as we drove south, passing vineyards brimming with muscatel grapes that cost us 1/5d (7p) for a couple of pounds.

Lunel is about 10 miles north east of Montpellier; we found this side of the South of France more attractive than the Côte d'Azur. We visited Nîmes with all its incredible old buildings, buying a card which entitled us to enter all the Roman sites. After climbing up steps and through luscious gardens we toiled to the top of the Tower Magnum where we had a fine view over the town; then into the wonderful Temple supposed to be the most intact of any Roman one anywhere, with its strong Greek influence. The arena is used now for bullfighting, but is smaller than the one in Rome though it has as many tiers. These wonderful buildings are incredibly well preserved – we drove over the Pont du Gard as high and long as the Brunel bridge over the River Tamar at Saltash. They have built a sort of replica the other side to strengthen it as, unlike ours, it is from Roman days.

The Colt Saloon was a popular stop for holidaymakers, being close to the route from Italy via France to Spain. It was a copy of a cowboy ranch; the stage – appropriately called La Boîte – was much too small for us and the opening night was beset with the usual anguish. The waiters were dressed as cowboys, and the audience sat in wagons all around or on cowhide-covered chairs. There was only one dressing room for all the artistes.

I remember a very nice and helpful stage manager and an attractive lady singer–dancer who turned out to have been a man quite recently. She was very pleased with the new parts she'd acquired and the lack of others, and not at all shy! We discovered a bar in the courtyard afterwards where there was quite a gathering of such fellows. It was all quite new to us.

The nearest beach to bathe from was at Grand du Roi. It had apartments in white concrete buildings behind, looking like large chests of drawers with balconies, new to us then but now one sees even larger atrocities built to overlook most tourist beaches. Everyone had departed to

> Geneva *La Suisse*: 'Certain numbers are excellent; this is particularly the case with Emerson & Jayne with their amusing parody Hindu of flying carpet, snakes, ribbons and flags – a joyful Fantasy!'

the balconies for lunch and we had a flat sandy beach and a sea with hardly a ripple all to ourselves. The diamonds on it hurt our eyes! Jack bought a faded fluorescent beach ball in a shop on the quaint little harbour nearby. The season was nearly over and the tourists departing.

Autumn 1966

Lunel to Geneva was not so far, and the 'Nights of Mystery' were very few, so Jack invited his father over to stay with him on the Geneva camp and I flew home to spend some time with Mama. Then, having no pantomime that year, we did two months at the Hansa again, helping the Christmas Stimmung with our candles.

We were invited to visit our magic friends the Coxes; we had admired his cocktail bar act at the Scala. In real life he was a policeman; we were treated to more magic and he conducted us through his magic den. A stout friend of his, a would-be magician who bought ready-made magical tricks, brought us flowers and persuaded me to show his wife Gisela how to disappear out of what looked like a telephone kiosk. I gathered I had to compress myself into a very small space to accomplish this trick and doubted whether Gisela had the right shape and flexibility for it – though she looked very good when he levitated her as if she was on her coffin.

It is strange how difficult it is to get into the best theatres in one's own country; only foreign acts are acceptable. Some excellent German acts never appear at the Hansa and yet might be seen at the Palladium, and vice versa. There was an occasion when we heard that we were being considered for a long-running show at the Victoria Palace after the end of a summer season we'd done with Ken Dodd in Torquay. We were very disappointed when we learned that another Oriental Act had been chosen; they had a good Eastern-sounding name (which we had not) and the Hylton hierarchy knew that I had once shed the role of Ballet Mistress to *Paint your Wagon* in order to become part of Emerson & Jayne.

Very soon after, we became friends with this act, Kazbek and Zari, who turned out to be Denis Williams and partner doing an excellent and dangerous looking whip act at the Hansa and other venues in Europe. We met several times and Jack kept up correspondence with Denis.

Athens 1967

After a month at home we started off again to perform in an Athens night club called the Copacabana. By the end of the month we had concluded that it would have been far better to have been there as tourists than on business! We didn't like the Lokal, or the owner who made it his business to cheat each artiste in some way or another. My brother had once attended a medical conference in Athens, and had experienced this sort of behaviour in his hotel. However none of this mattered when the sun shone and we lived beside the orange trees. we met a retired naval man, Captain Coke, and his wife camping opposite us in their large motor caravan, and we have remained friends to this day.

We spent our free time admiring the Parthenon and its like, travelling as far as possible up hills, and to the numerous islands. We felt so lucky to be paid the equivalent of £100 for all this, and I was persuaded to buy a light-coloured mink coat – a wicked deed for a vegetarian to perpetrate, but I loved its soft cosiness and hoped it looked like artificial fur. Today, I dare not take it out of the cupboard. Later that year we had bookings in Switzerland and France with contracts for Finland and Oslo in the summer after the free months at home.

> Helsinki *Paivan Sanomat*:
> 'The secret of the flying carpet will cause sleepless
> nights for all those who visit the July show at the
> Peacock. A couple of cobras and a couple called
> Emerson & Jayne present a crazy and exciting act
> masterfully.'

Outside Helsinki, we gazed at the midnight sun through the trees. The
place we were to work in was very civilised: Linnenmeki – a large theatre
in what would nowadays be called a Theme Park. The place seemed to
have other attractions besides our variety show with acts doing amazing
stunts, often in the open air – or maybe the gentleman in a bowler hat,
swaying dangerously at the top of a very high slender pole he'd climbed,
could not have fitted the latter and his hat under the ceiling indoors. In one
pavilion, we watched chubby little girls walking up a steep spiral slope on
large balls – this looked very difficult.

The lady in charge of our show was extremely courteous and put on a
fine dinner party for the company before it was time for us to depart.

We spent the next month at a proper theatre in Oslo called Le Chat Noir.

> Oslo *Aften Posten*:
> 'I must maintain that Emerson & Jayne represent the
> high spot in the show, with their gay and very effective
> play with their Magic Carpet.'

We were treated to a trip down a fjord in a steamer by the management.
After all this time only a few impressions remain; our tent in the sun on
the top slope of the camp, a ski run on the distant slope opposite, waiting
for the wintersport snow, the King of Norway standing on the deck of his
yacht down in the harbour.

Oslo began with two days of tribulation. If you have unusual music
like ours, and you don't get in the queue at the beginning of the band call,
you've had it! The sexy girl climbing out of a shell being lit to her
advantage and seemingly doing an 'end of term' dance cost us our proper
rehearsal and the result was chaos. The next day, to appease us, the band
promised us we'd rehearse after the final rehearsal. The third night things
went a little better, though the orchestra was still out to win the Grand
National.

After two nights at the harbour we camped among birches and firs
with the water below us. I woke early and went to pick wild raspberries

for breakfast – so late compared with ours; here still growing – and they were delicious. There were many more people in Oslo than in Helsinki and they looked very English. Of course, we did have a Viking invasion once to get us mixed up. The shops down in the town weren't very exciting, apart from those selling woollen sweaters with the attractive patterned shoulders. We bought a nice vase to put my first-night bouquet in and eyed an attractive silvered lampshade, planning to carry it off home at the end of the run.

Nancy

After Oslo it was Paris and Switzerland again, mostly return visits to places we'd performed at before. Thence to spend Christmas in Nancy; anyone who has visited this town will know how gracious it is. We were to be included in a Dickensian-type operetta at the Municipal Theatre, which stood in a square of fine buildings dating from the time of Louis XV. It was statelier than any other theatre or opera house we have ever had the pleasure of performing in.

We were to appear as a dream or apparition at the awakening of the miser in *Les Cloches de Corneville*. Obviously our Paris agent had considered we might fit the bill, but we could tell that having seen our props, costumes and music, the producer was very dubious and annoyed they had been sent a mere variety act! However, having struggled through the first show without too much of the usual chaos, we gathered that we

> Leicester *Mercury*: 'Emerson & Jayne's fluorescent snake charming and their Magic Carpet fitted perfectly into the Eastern theme and held the audience spellbound.'

had gone up in their estimation, and we were able to enjoy their respect for the duration. Even the orchestra came up trumps with those sections that required some improvisation from the percussion.

We did not live in the van those two months but in lodgings where we had a charming landlady. We always found the French to be much more sympathetic in the provinces than in Paris.

Leicester

Al Heath, an English agent we'd worked for in the past, asked us to take part in the pantomime he was putting on at the de Montfort Hall in Leicester the following Christmas. I was delighted, as we could live at home with Mama, though we knew that she, being somewhat of a snob, was not too happy to broadcast to her bridge partners that her daughter would be appearing in the Leicester pantomime. I had hoped that, as the de Montfort Hall was the usual venue for concerts or ballet, we would be considered legitimate. Some younger members of the family came to see us, but I don't believe Mama ever did. I was told that, due to the difficulty of keeping daylight out of the vast area during matinées, our black-light effects were not completely effective.

It was not a good stage or auditorium for other than concerts and ballets, being much too barren and without atmosphere but, as with the Ballets Jooss at the Opera House, it gave me a glow of satisfaction to be performing in my birthplace to my friends.

Autumn 1969

Midge at the piano

We advertised Ovaltine around English theatres and took part in John Redgrave's show in Scarborough before catching the boat for Dublin where we were to take part in the panto at the Gaiety Theatre. It's a nice old theatre with bills on the foyer walls going back to 1815.

Although we had been there twice with the Ballets Jooss, I didn't remember the interior, though we both remembered the fleas we caught.

Jack was 55 that January and I was 54 in March. Twoosy, Midge's piano-playing daughter, was six months. 'I never thought I'd make it,' sighed Jack over the Sunday paper.

We enjoyed that season immensely (as we did a following one), though we were not sure that we suited either subject, one being *The Pied Piper of Hamelin* and the other *Little Red Riding Hood*. The audience appreciated us, the orchestra with its lady conductor was excellent, and the cast headed by the popular Maureen Potter was kind and friendly towards us, and we would all gather in the crowded bar-cum-green-room for drinks after the evening show.

Eamonn Andrews was taller and less square and schoolboyish in the face than we'd imagined. Anyway, he came to the show and we had a little chat afterwards; he congratulated us.

We lived that season out at the country club at Port Marnock which belonged to him. Port Marnock was a beautiful site looking right over the bay but we had to bus the seven miles into Dublin each day.

We used to try a different hotel every weekend to laze in and read the Sunday papers. One Sunday, we landed up at the Shelbourne, where the Springboks were staying. They were all dithering around in our corridor as someone had planted a parcel by their rooms with a loud ticking noise emanating from it. We hoped it was only a joke. We were rather shocked to find that we had to pay 173/6 (£8.68) exclusive of breakfast at 15/- (75p) and 12% service. These days that sounds rather cheap for a swish hotel!

At last we learned that we were to finish on 28 February as Jack Benny was booked in on 7 March. Meanwhile, we were playing to packed houses, though for some reason I felt a bit depressed – I don't know why. There was no reason for it as life was good – lots of lovely praise, a beautiful site for the van with bath, electricity and a private beach with dunes, and only two matinées to go!

Jack was worried as we still hadn't found his father a new London flat to move into, and before we were leaving for Teheran in March; we also had an offer for Israel. All the inflammatory places!

We visited the magnificent Phoenix Park and its zoo; the real purpose of the visit. Jack wanted to make an elephant to open the Act instead of our routine with the umbrellas and boojums. He planned to work the legs somehow from inside it; it was to have our carpet over it and the snake basket on top of that. I hoped I could enter on my own legs!

1970

We had a contract from a Greek agent who, we learnt, had worked in Iran for thirty-three years. The trip was a great disappointment and a great worry. We left England in chilly weather spending too much time in Beirut and Amman Airports which seemed like those in a Graham Greene novel – lavatory doors sticking, pipes broken and Jordanians lounging everywhere.

We were escorted to our hotel by two gentlemen who had had to wait two hours for our late incoming plane. They told us that the next day was a public holiday and everything – including the Lido where we were to work – would be closed. We therefore looked forward to exploring the town, though we would have liked to deposit our equipment into the Lido safely.

The next day, after appreciating our private bathroom in the hotel, and window shopping the attractive Persian wares, we did our usual nerve-racking première on a stage completely unsuitable for a black-light act. The next day we were told that, owing to the holiday being over, people had no money to visit the theatre, and would we perform at their Moulin Rouge as well, later at night for no extra pay. They obviously had no money either. Of course we refused as this was not in our contract and told the agent, who escorted us to the bosses who obviously wanted to get their money's worth. They also asked us to move to an apartment (with no refrigerator) which would be cheaper than the hotel. Then they cancelled all the shows for the next seven days.

The management office was full of dark, unsmiling men. They had three cinemas with night clubs attached, and a score of minions typing and carrying tiny cups of tea around. We were given some tea but never introduced to anyone. Jack said to the Greek agent: 'We may be English, but we certainly aren't fools.' It was like a scene straight out of Kafka – they kept retiring for little Persian chats before bargaining afresh. We had the return fare, but they had our passports which were necessary for them to obtain our exit permits as we had done one show.

We then went to the British Consul who advised us to try and come to an arrangement as they were 'very proud people and resented other nationals'. Somehow our agent managed to obtain our passports for us and we decided, rather reluctantly on Jack's part, to escape. This we achieved with the help of a friendly stagehand who, at the crack of dawn, unlocked the theatre where our props had been hidden by the management, so that we could load them into our getaway taxi.

At the station, I recognised a porter carrying our heavy crate on his back; I had seen him around at the theatre and he gave us a wonderful smile of approval, which I can see to this day.

Pantomime 1970–71

In those days pantomime lasted a goodly chunk of the year, and artistes thought themselves fortunate to be included in one, escaping travel and tucked away in cosy warm dressing rooms if they were lucky. One Nottingham pantomime with Barbara Windsor as Aladdin lasted until Easter – unheard of these days!

Our second visit to Sunderland was the first with the larger Carpet. We had had a popular Northern star lead the first time, the 'Little Waster', and manager Jack Brennan had put the show on with mostly a northern cast. In those days Jack usually played a very commanding Slave and I was the Fairy, roles which somehow tied in to the oriental style of our Act.

Stories from Paris

We would always try and get our two parents to wherever it was feasible for them to travel, neither of them being sprightly any more. After a stroke in the '60s, and later terrible attacks of trigeminal neuralgia, Mama was far from sturdy; Allen was lame, and lonely in his deafness. He loved coming to Paris and we would lodge him in a hotel in Suresne on the opposite side of the river, from where he would descend on us in the morning – far too early after our late hours of work!

We were all great fans of Jacques Tati and went to see his film *Traffic* which we enjoyed as much as his previous ones. Ironically, it was rather difficult getting to the cinema that day as there was a metro and bus strike on. We also saw a documentary made by the Nazis about the occupation of France; the French were flocking in to see it and we were amazed at how fully they seemed to have collaborated with the Germans.

What was to have been our last free day in Paris was taken up with a TV shoot. At last the contract was signed; it was as French as French can be and probably gave them permission to print the Emerson & Jayne film as many times as they wished. We hoped we'd even get a copy for ourselves! The only sure thing was the fee – FF10,000 for us and FF1,000 for the agent who should have thought herself very lucky, as she was off in Spain rather than being around to negotiate for us and avoid the pitfalls.

We found out later that the TV film had been shown in Germany and was shot by a German company, not a French one as we had supposed, and has not yet been shown on French TV. Later though, we were shown the film taken at the Olympia; disappointing, as white light had to be used instead of ultraviolet – fluorescent colours tend to overexpose and look pale instead of vivid. On the whole we found our Act less commercial than we'd expected – in fact I thought I looked too lightweight and the Act, on the whole, too 'fey'. We decided we'd have to pull our socks down! Jack was interested to see his animated objects from the front and was quite impressed at their realism, particularly as he'd been working under difficulties, trying to keep out of the beams of about seven white spotlights. The film was not too bad really and our haggishness less obvious on a TV screen. The promoters seemed quite pleased with it anyway and we certainly get a good introduction (in German) for the show: 'Never before seen on TV *etc etc*'!

Paris Olympia Magic Show

We shared the theatre with a production of *Jesus Christ Superstar* – he was supposedly magical too! We would appear after him and also in a few matinées and a day off when Paul McCartney came with the Beatles for a gala night. The star of our show was a gentleman who performed various feats, including lifting gigantic-looking weights. We were most intrigued to discover with a little espionage that he used magnets for some effects, as Jack did on some of our props.

Here we got a rather dubious compliment from the gentleman who had arranged our first Dortmund date and wanted to manage us from then on. He told us that we were the best thing in the show but why had we not received a good notice in the press? I tried to explain that we liked to get home to bed instead of drinking with the folk in the bar, which was necessary for good press notices. One never could get Jack to parties unless he knew friends would be there, and then he would not linger long.

He always preferred to spend time making things, rather than being sociable.

As soon as we arrived home, my sister phoned to tell me to get to Leicester where Mama had collapsed whilst playing bridge and had been taken to a nursing home. I watched her fading away until her death that August, aged 84.

Magic

Jack and I were contracted to yet another Magic show in the Hamburg Opperettenhaus in September, and then one in Margate.

Letter to Jack's Father:

> Getting to Hamburg was like magic – we drove to Harwich and the boat did the rest, docking within two minutes' drive from the theatre. The *Operetten* folk were still rehearsing for their tour, so we had to wait until the next day to unload. The weather turned cooler and we were glad of the warmth from our gas light. We both flopped as the result of sudden inactivity, I particularly after nursing Mama and, perhaps sub-consciously, dropping the act of trying to prove my worth in the role of youngest daughter.

After the magic shows in Hamburg we returned to Margate. The Margate Magic show went off quite well, though I must say it was a hell of a lot of work for one day. We didn't get back to Stanford till around 3am. We then loaded up and made for Paris for two months at Le Milliardaire.

We now had for the first time, the complete nudity which had for some years been customary at the Crazy Horse. l don't know whether the departure of the G-string makes stripping less cheap. Certainly sculpture is more dignified without fig leaves!

I wrote above about Jack's reluctance to mingle long at theatrical gatherings of 'bonhomie' and he himself remarked once that we knew more people in Paris than we did in our village of Stanford. We had seldom worked with our Parisian friends in England, and seldom met English magician friends abroad. The last time we returned to Paris, we shared one of those new dressing rooms with Danny Ray, who had taken part in the Magic Circle Show at the Scala where we had appeared. I often see those legs of his table disappearing in my mind! I correspond with his widow each Christmas. The Gentys were nearly permanent fixtures in the cabaret, and took part in an Edinburgh Festival show. We noticed faded earlier posters, when up there for pantomime once – then there were the

Baladins, and the black-light act Omar Pasha, removing a poor fellow's head and putting it back, an act he inherited from the original Sambalo.

There was the immaculate Vendryes, a Dane I believe; we performed again with him in Spain later. We repeatedly ran into the magician Phoa Yan Tiong, and of course Pifar, a fine acrobat and close friend of our agent Carmen.

Lastly, there was a tall Frenchman who, on our very first night at this strange new locale, seemed to resent any allocation of space to new arrivals. This was Julian who stood with his back to the audience upstage and seemed to receive embraces from arms mysteriously disembodied. I hasten to write that on subsequent meetings, he and his wife couldn't have been more charming and friendly.

We left on the newly instituted Folkestone car ferry, so saving the drive over Dover Hill. The French roads were so bad that we reached Paris only just in time to prepare our act for the show. We found Le Milliardaire in a dreadful state of builders' mess, they were busy turning what we called the Catacombs into air-conditioned dressing rooms. Meanwhile, conditions were worse than ever! It must have cost a fortune and we were rather surprised that Mme P at last had noticed there was room for improvement round behind!

This time at Le Milliardaire, the stripping part of the show was much less artistic, the choreography having been taken over by a new Italian couple. The girls were very pretty but the repetitive movements they were given were of only very basic interest. There were times when we thought we might bring friends to see a show, but I regret to say that this show did not warrant it.

Egypt 1973

Off we set on another grand trip into the unknown. We had a month's contract at the Auberge des Pyramides outside Cairo. It really lived up to its name, standing alone in the midst of the desert with the Pyramids just along the narrow land ahead of us.

We were introduced to some gentlemen sitting in the palm-treed courtyard of the establishment whom we surmised were our employers. They welcomed us very politely but we noticed that we had arrived in the middle of some serious conversation, which they quickly resumed.

We watched a mediocre cabaret that night consisting of a ballet and a singer. We were surprised when suddenly, through the midst of the dancers, an apparition appeared with draped winglike arms and floated about among the group. We were completely astounded in recognising Michael Charnley, a dancer in our time with the Ballets Jooss (he had

THE
INTERNATIONAL
BROTHERHOOD
OF
MAGICIANS
BRITISH RING No. 25

presents

★★

GRAND INTERNATIONAL GALA OF MAGIC

★★

WINTER GARDENS —— MARGATE
GENERAL MANAGER & LICENSEE
JACK GREEN.

SATURDAY 30th SEPTEMBER, 1972.
5 p.m. & 8.30 p.m.

The Programme

arranged by

WM. G.

STICKLAND

STAGE MANAGER
(for BRITISH RING I.B.M.)

PAUL GRAHAM

Assistant
Stage Managers
BARRY MILLER
DAVID JORDAN

danced as the Young Soldier to my Young Girl). He went on to become a very good choreographer and was well known in the dance world; we never found out how he landed up in Cairo in that company and we had no opportunity of asking him as he avoided us that night, and later circumstances prevented any chance of a meeting. We felt concerned for him, and were later sorry to hear that he had died.

The next day, we learnt that we would not be fulfilling our engagement at the Auberge, as Egypt was at war! It was the Yom Kippur War, and for a few days we were kept rather in suspense as no one seemed to know what next, and we wondered – not without anxiety – what it was all about. We were determined to go along and see the Pyramids and our houseboy volunteered to accompany us. We also explored Cairo and found the natives very hospitable, plying us with small cups of very black coffee. In the kitchen where we cooked I opened the fridge, but shut it again very quickly when I saw rows of tiny little feathered dead birds where one usually kept the eggs.

It was not long before we were sitting in a ramshackle old bus, a fat Arab in his robes beside us and our heavy cases strapped onto the roof. We bumped along through desert roads all day and into the night, dropping off to sleep, until a particularly horrendous bump woke us all, landing me on the fat Arab's lap. The driver must have nodded off too because, on clambering out, we found we were in middle of a rocky piece of desert! Amazingly enough, our theatrical possessions were still on the top of the bus.

We finally reached Benghazi and civilisation, where we would catch a plane home. We had seen the Nile, the Pyramids and where the Battle of El Alamein was fought.

As Jack put it in a letter to his father: 'Our Eastern contracts are always liable to subsidence!'

Winter and Summer 1975

Before long we were off to The Pavilion Theatre in Bournemouth. Again it was Derek Salberg's *Aladdin*, though the cast was entirely different this time. We had Roy Castle starring as Wishee Washee, and the late Jack Tripp, 'surely one of the great dames of British pantomime today', as a critic rightly wrote, adding – dare I write conceitedly – that 'Emerson & Jayne were one of the best additions seen in pantomimes at the Pavilion.'

Unfortunately Jack's father fell ill during the run and Jack had to travel to London several times to attend to his welfare. He had the usual chesty winter complaint that this time got the better of him; Jack got him to hospital where sadly he died. I see his gaze on that day as he lay in bed and we stood waving goodbye at the door of the room before our return

PAVILION THEATRE
BOURNEMOUTH

Entertainments Manager for Bournemouth Corporation: SAMUEL J. BELL   Box Office Tel. 25061

COMMENCING SATURDAY, DECEMBER 22nd, FOR A SEASON
From Tues. Jan. 8th to Sat. Feb. 9th Nightly 7.30
Mats. Wed., Thurs. & Sat. 2.30
Special Saturday Morning Mats. at 10.30 a.m.
Jan. 19th, 26th & Feb. 2nd & 9th

DEREK SALBERG presents

ROY CASTLE ★

IN

ALADDIN

WITH

JACK TRIPP

ALLEN CHRISTIE   DENNIS SPENCER
DAVID AND TONY WEBB ★ WENDY SMITH
JANE HARROD   DEREK HOLT

★ **EMERSON & JAYNE** AND THEIR MAGIC CARPET ★

CURRIE'S FANTASTIC VOLCANIC ERUPTION

Pantomime Directed by FRANK ADEY   Choreography by JANE HARROD

PRICES STALLS & CIRCLE £1.10, £1.00, 90p REAR STALLS 70p
Children ex. Wed. Dec. 26th Sat. Afternoons & Evenings
STALLS & CIRCLE 60p, 55p, 45p REAR STALLS 40p
OAP's at Children's rate Wed. & Thurs. mats from 9th Jan.
Concession for Parties of 20 or more adults (ex. Wed. Dec. 26th & Sats.)

BOOK NOW Box Office open Weekdays 10 a.m. to 8.30 p.m. Tel: 25061

PROVISIONAL BOOKING FORM
ALADDIN

Box Office:
PAVILION THEATRE, BOURNEMOUTH.   Date _____

Please reserve _____ (qty.) seats in Stalls/Circle at _____ each

Date of Performance _____   Eve/Mat. _____

NAME (Block Letters) _____

ADDRESS _____

Telephone No. _____
If Remittance enclosed – £   p   (Total)   Please enclose S.A.E.
G. & H. Organ, Wilegan, Bristol.

to the theatre; the forlornness and acceptance of finality in his eyes still haunts me.

Barney Colehan's *The Good Old Days* had now been in existence for twenty-one years and so had our Act. It seemed therefore very appropriate

that we should take part in the BBC TV show Barney was putting on in March 1974.

This we did before setting off for almost three months in Madrid. Of our visit, Sydney Vaunce wrote in *The Stage* May 1974: 'Gibraltar may rock but artistes do not seem to be unwelcome in Madrid'.

Work was a large, most pleasant cabaret restaurant in the Florida Park there, seemingly quite new and modelled on the Paris Lido style.

Barney Colehan

A large ballet was being rehearsed when we arrived and there were several acts, including the Three Monarchs, a well known English comedy musical group. We got to know Cedric from the trio, as we shared a dressing room and together went on an expedition to Franco's grave and memorial.

By this time we had a new and very roomy Leyland lorry with a custom-built body different from its predecessor in that the whole exterior could open in two parts like a great stable door so that we could drive a minivan up ramps into the interior. Of course if we were transporting the Large Carpet Act, one of us would have to drive this mini on the road (as we had been used to doing with the Isetta) but the new lorry was so much easier for loading and, when parked in pleasant surroundings as we often were, what a wonderful open verandah it provided for basking on!

Pantomime 1974–75

This was at the Birmingham Hippodrome with Larry Grayson as the lead, of whom a critic wrote:

It falls of course to Larry Grayson to be the central support,

but he then went on to say:

The most unexpected novelty perhaps is Alfred Marks whose talents easily encompass an Abenazer full of majesty at one moment and an abject cringer at another. He brings a new dimension to the part and threatens to steal the show . . . One of the most popular delights is Keith

Driving the minivan out of the Leyland lorry

Harris and Cuddles, his impertinent and likeable dummy . . . In a story where the rub of a lamp can produce a genie, there should be no surprise at a magic carpet, yet it is impossible to watch the expertise of Emerson & Jayne without wonderment. There before your eyes, they appear to reproduce in fact what you have only read in fantasy.

It was the first time we had been in the same show as Alfred Marks, and we had always admired his performances in earlier comical TV series. I talked to him as he sat in the wings wearing his turban and thought what a nice man he was!

It is hard to believe that we were able to secrete ourselves and our van right in the middle of busy Birmingham down by the canal in a hidden corner where we stayed undisturbed right through that panto season.

Later on in the year we flew to Israel to perform in a small theatre at the side of the larger concert hall in Haifa whose audience would visit us after their show.

In contrast to the landlord of the *pension* who had observed that we were 'over the hill', the theatre owner was very nice and polite to us and we were honoured to be invited to a feast where his baby son was to be circumcised.

We enjoyed Haifa, its climate and its people, and found a matey taxi driver who served as an excellent courier for our excursions. He even showed us

The Magic Carpet emerging from the Leyland

where Christ walked on the water and how to split a large sunflower seed open between the teeth! We had the most exciting day wandering through the ruins of the Masada camp, awed by the thoughts of its tragic history. It was very hot up there in the sandy terrain, and we were glad to get down to the lake in spite of it being warm; it was so salty that one could float without sinking, to cure ones arthritis *etc*!

Summer 1975

Jack enjoyed making advertisements for us and he had quite a flair for composing rather unusual ones, as he had with most things! He advertised once or twice a year in *The Stage*, hoping it might bring us an attractive offer of work. After one of our sessions up the Eiffel Tower, he wrote the following advertisement:

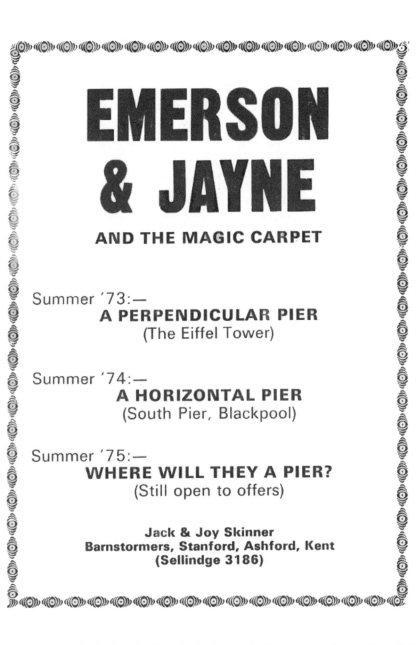

EMERSON & JAYNE

AND THE MAGIC CARPET

Summer '73:—
A PERPENDICULAR PIER
(The Eiffel Tower)

Summer '74:—
A HORIZONTAL PIER
(South Pier, Blackpool)

Summer '75:—
WHERE WILL THEY A PIER?
(Still open to offers)

Jack & Joy Skinner
Barnstormers, Stanford, Ashford, Kent
(Sellindge 3186)

I always had the feeling it had resulted in one of our Scottish pantomimes!

One advertisement definitely ensured that we would never receive contracts through any of the leading English Agencies! Jack had the cheek to thank them in print for leaving him free to accept all the lucrative foreign offers instead of theirs!

Indeed, work in England usually arose from other sources; from those folk who had seen the Act's potential for panto, and theatre managers such as Richard Condon, Al Heath, Jimmy Logan, John Redgrave, Johnny Riscoe, Derek and Keith Salberg, Evelyn Taylor and Sonny Zahl to name but a few.

Had we been engaged frequently by leading agents in large English shows such as those at the Palladium, we would never have been happy, as we would have not been granted enough time to do justice to the Act. Naturally the stars were guaranteed many more minutes' exposure than a mere Speciality Act demanding ten minutes to tell a fairy story in black-lit mime.

No one clamoured for our 'ten minutes' that summer, so we accepted an offer to return to the Florida Park's Restaurante Espectaculo in the Paseo del Coches del Retiro. The cast turned out to be entirely different from last season, consisting of the Trotter Brothers, The Ricards from the Paris Lido, the Briac Ballet, and us.

It was about then that we moved into our converted barn from the bungalow opposite. Our local builder and carpenter, John Wood, had done a wonderful job to Jack's design and we were able to witness the last skilled touches of Ron the carpenter. We decided to let the bungalow to holiday visitors.

Norwich 1976

Norwich was always a super place to perform in, and we visited the city with its beautiful cathedral, colourful market, and lovely museum, several times.

We were there with the Ballets Jooss when, I recall, we were shown a fine bed of mushrooms which a stage manager was cultivating under the stage! We visited again later after some improvements had been made to the theatre structure; I forgot to ask what had happened to the mushrooms.

We participated in *Aladdin* twice in Norwich. Both times we were able to live conveniently and comfortably right on the spot in our motor caravan.

This time, we had John Inman as our top and very pleasant company which included Ken Barnes, David Davenport, Paul & Barry Harman, Yvonne Marsh, and a sealion who lived close to us on the car park!

My brother sent us a cutting from the *Leicester Evening Mercury* headed 'Mr Leicester's DIARY'. 'Leicester born Joy Skinner and her husband Jack are proving a great attraction at Norwich's Theatre Royal where their optical illusion act features in the pantomime Aladdin'. It then went on to praise the act and state that we had the biggest applause of the evening from the 1,200 strong audiences *etc*! Our heads swelled; we wondered who had been talking to the press. As a result of the piece, many old friends came to see the show and looked us up. Hugh Jenkins, then Minister for the Arts, also came; we guessed the theatre had asked for a grant.

We did not leave Norwich after loading the last night, as we wanted to see *Green Table* performed by the Tanz Forum of Cologne who followed us at the theatre. We thought they gave a better interpretation of it than the Joffrey ballet. Their Death was very good, as was the Spy. The Old Mother was not tired and brittle enough, nor the Young Girl frail and clear enough in movement. The accompaniment on tape did not give as good an atmosphere as our two pianos had done.

Home Again and On

The Burkes had escaped the gunfire of Beirut, where they had been working in charge of the Casino show. They hoped the war would soon be over so that they could return. We were to spend only a short time at Barnstormers, for we were due in Geneva at the beginning of March.

We had time to go and see Jimmy Jewell in *The Comedian* in London. We had never seen him in a straight play before and were most impressed with his performance.

About this time Angela Baddeley died. She had always been so popular in the plays I was taken to in my youth, when Hermione Gingold was also around. The latter quipped: 'I miss her baddeley'. I wouldn't have registered this so strongly had it not been pronounced in mirth for a friendly reason.

We were looking forward to getting back to Switzerland that March and we tried a new camp not so far out of town. It was in the woods along the Arve River and, being out of season, nice and private. But as for working conditions – what an anticlimax after our lovely great stage in Norwich!

We were supposed to be booked at Pussy Cat, the best nightclub in Geneva – it may have been for the clientèle, but it certainly wasn't for us. The stage was minute and the stage management hopeless, the show twice nightly and all artistes in one dressing room. We should have guessed what it would be like from its name. The audience was as ghastly as you'd expect from what was almost a brothel. We never reached home till 3am; it's not surprising that all foreign artistes had to go for a thorough medical.

Fortunately, the audience for the foreign acts got better when the Motor Show opened in town, and the months passed quite quickly. Towards the end of our stay, we got an offer to join the Little Angels of Korea on their trip to South Africa at $1000 a week, but had to refuse as it ran into our next pantomime date which was to be up in Sunderland again.

Hong Kong

On 27 August a hire car took us to Heathrow whence we were to fly to Hong Kong. Twoosey, the remaining little poodle, thought this smart car very fine and hastily jumped in to take possession. She was to be left again, poor little mite, though Thorpe would take her for lovely walks in our absence.   The trip took twenty-two hours, the boredom broken by those little trays of identical (vegetarian) food – rather nauseating the fourth time round.

We touched down at Muscat, Calcutta and Rangoon on the way; some hotel staff were at the airport to welcome us finally at Hong Kong.

We were to stay at the Excelsior, containing the large Convention Theatre where we were to appear. The Excelsior was the highest building in Hong Kong at that time, though photographs these days show a sea of many such giants!

I wrote to my brother soon after we'd arrived in Hong Kong:

> This is an enormous complex Trust House Forte sold to Hong Kong Land. The Convention Centre has 38 floors – 4 floors of offices, and 34 floors of hotel. They tried to dock us four days' pay, as the baggage had stayed at Heathrow, but Jack wrote one of his sly letters pointing out that he had wanted the boxes to travel with us on our plane as part of the contract. We got it all in the end!
>
> The typhoon was just over when we arrived and families were mourning their dead as a result of the landslides. We were told that they have to appease the anger of the dead peoples' spirits before burying them. How can they be consoled if flattened by mud?

Our luxurious room looked over the harbour crowded with sampans, and we were able to watch two old men in English naval uniform, under the Union Jack, ring the bell every half hour and operate the Midday Gun – all so British, and all now in the past.

Although we had the usual rehearsal, orchestral and staging problems, the staff couldn't have tried harder to put us at our ease. What a contrast to some stagehands we have had to rely on. Even the attractive little room maid had the most endearing manners not unlike a puppy or kitten that rolls over to be tickled when it catches sight of you!

Our theatre baggage arrived, only a week after us, having remained at Heathrow freight department in spite of our efforts to despatch it a fortnight before. The management had to prolong the stay of a previous artiste in consequence, while we had the opportunity to explore this exciting Island.

On 8 September the sampans in the harbour flew little red flags at half mast in honour of Mau who had died at midnight. We had been up a steep hill to be interviewed by an English lady for the *South China News* and looked down at busy harbour.

We had never seen so many people crowding the streets and tiny shops as down in the town in that humid heat. The buses poured hot fumes out of great Leyland engines and we discovered it was better to take a tram than a bus for cooler air! I looked up at characters formed by moving lights; I thought it press news, but they were actually advertising the film *All the President's Men*. The name Nixon passed along it and Jack explained to me what later became known as 'Watergate'. I often wonder how Nixon felt at the disgrace, and was he really the culprit or just the scapegoat?

What idyllic landscape around us; we trammed the length and breadth of it. It was as beautiful as Rio and not unlike Scandinavian fjords. We certainly enjoyed the hours we were not on stage. We went to real China by bus but immediately found the atmosphere was far from friendly.

On our free day we would take the tram or travel round extreme hairpin bends in a bus to Silvermine Bay, where we could swim out to a raft and bask awhile when the sea was flat.

One day there was a tornado and the sea breakers were so high they would have dashed us over had we tried to get beyond them!

We took a bus into Kowloon and visited a large Chinese Arts and Crafts shop not far from the frontier. Our agent Carmen had asked us to bring her back some hand-embroidered sheets. We bought these and some lovely silk shirts for us – also with embroidery – very inexpensively, undoubtedly produced by slave labour. We noticed also a very different atmosphere among the personnel in the shop, as if they disliked us.

We drove further into China past endless paddyfields where men were almost up to their waists in mud, picking up worms which they threw into their wide brimmed hats. Their hovels of huts behind looked so pathetic with the odd scraggy chicken in a tiny cage outside, waiting to be eaten. We were shown round a village on the route but Canton, the nearest town, was too far to visit.

At last it was time to leave. After travelling first class on the eight-hour trip to Bombay we found ourselves overnighting there as the plane broke down. So we visited Gandhi's house much to Jack's pleasure because, as a boy, he had once met him in England and procured his autograph The Indians happened to be celebrating what would have been Gandhi's 105th birthday!

Paris again

Our next journey was back to Paris to climb the Eiffel Tower agian. It was very hot; as we truggled up and down the Tower, there was not a whiff of breeze and not a cloud in the sky – in fact the only draught we met was one of almost liquid fire as we passed through the kitchens to our dressing room.

This time we got our Act on without too much difficulty, and the orchestra still remembered our music. The lighting and stage management departments also remembered us from two years ago. We were both a bit stiff after not working for three months, but that was to be expected. We'd already met many friends and acquaintances up on the Tower, as well as our Swiss friends who lived in a motorcaravan they'd made themselves from an army truck. It was often parked on the Champs de Mars when we arrived; we though they lived there and they thought we lived there! They were a middle-aged couple, she an artist and he a philosopher of some strange science. They later found their way to park a night in front of Barnstormers and we have corresponded ever since.

We had bought a new snake-charming instrument in China called the 'erhoo' – it looked rather like a croquet mallet. Jack was quite sure it

Our menagerie

would do justice to my playing – or rather my snake-charming abilities. Jack always overestimated my musical skills, knowing I could read notes after many wasted piano lessons at school and at home. A recorder, yes, but not something that made strange unrecognisable sounds! However, the erhoo looked oriental and weird, as befitted the Act, and had its première in Paris at Le Milliardaire.

Jack had been working on another embellishment to our act – a cheeky little red bird not unlike a robin; its predecessor had flown on to my flute and just looked into it without further ado, but this new fellow had moving eyes and, having seen a tiny wormlike snake lying inside the erhoo, to my surprise, digs it out with his beak and carries it off. There is still a slightly larger-sized snake asleep in my erhoo;

he wakes as a result of the breezy scramble and odd notes, then climbs out and wiggles off to the safety of the parents' basket. The snakes provided a nice laugh for the further animals' antics – that is if the audience was interested in watching, not always the case in a nightclub!

We were asked if we would go to Florida for three months to take part in a magic show. Why couldn't these people make their attractive offers earlier? Alas, we were signed up for panto in Sunderland and that horrid Pussy Cat in Geneva.

Sunderland *Aladdin* 1976–77

At the Sunderland Empire, the cast was headed by Peter Goodwright, a very clever impressionist with a gentle turn of humour and sympathetic character. Other friends there included Don Smoothy from the old Variety days, whom we met in Oxford when he was a partner with Tommy Layton, John Wade, and Ward Allen; a ventriloquist with a nice goofy black dog and a crow. He is excellent but we 'speshes' are seldom popular with the leading roles as we take too much of their time on stage – though we never felt any antagonism from Peter.

We were on a great lorry park at the back of the theatre which was most convenient as we could serve now and then as a coffee house for friends and members of the cast.

Abanazer – John Wade – told us he had access to a school swimming pool, as he knew a member of the staff. We had a good swim but got chilled hanging around being sociable afterwards. The water wasn't all that well heated for arthritical dancers! Our dressing room walls were decorated with many cards and the theatre was packed every day with very voluble children – they adored it. Eric the stage manager brought his girlfriend to an egg and bean curry in the van, and we learnt quite a lot of company gossip. Apparently the show was too long as the comedians were spinning it out as usual and wanted the speciality acts to cut. One is never popular if one makes a good impression or is praised in earshot of a star. It may sound extremely bigheaded to recount what a leading comedian once told us – partly in fun – that he didn't want to be on the same bill as us ever again! Well, aren't all theatre artistes bigheaded, if we have the need to display our big heads on stage?

When we woke at Seaburn one morning the snow lay about six inches deep around us so we made our way back into town for another week of matinées, sometimes three shows in a day. We received another invitation to go swimming and this time the water was sufficiently warm. The

schoolteacher vicar came back to lunch in the van and we regaled him with a Bloody Mary, cheese flan and vegetables.

After he left we enjoyed our Sunday papers and tried to watch Larry Grayson on our portable TV; also Esther Rantzen exploring injustices – rather unsuccessfully, owing to bad reception. We went to see George Lacy's Panto in Newcastle on February 14. He gave a very polished performance, which would have been perfect had he had a little more human charm. But he was over 70 and, like us, he was probably experiencing the aches and pains of aging. Jack remarked this part of the world was really a part of us, seeing that we had given our last performance with the Ballets Jooss in Newcastle in 1947 and performed here at Sunderland on several other occasions.

Our manager, Mr Todds, came and told us that Bill Robertson was interested in having us for Wimbledon next year if we were free. However, when he was rumoured to be in, of course we gave a bad show, as always seems to happen on these occasions. The fairy lights on my carpet never lit up and the rope descended to the ground before I ever got to climbing it. Such is life – I don't think we ever did that Wimbledon pantomime!

One night, we watched the first part of the show from the circle. It was packed with old dears, and I couldn't imagine we'd get much reaction to our Act. Peter Goodwright portrayed Wishee Washee as a backward schoolboy, not as himself! It was excellent rendering and had much work behind it.

Up the rope and on to the carpet

We went round the Vaux brewery which was near the theatre. It still had those marvellous great horses with hairy boots, pulling the drays driven by gentlemen in bowler hats. We were told the gases from the yeast fumes can be very dangerous to the men who clean the vats out, should they stay breathing over them too long. A dog walking with its head at floor level would be knocked out immediately. The theatre chaplain came to coffee in our dressing room. He was a nice little fellow who had the tact not to shove God down your throat all the time.

During the run, the cast was entertained in the town's beautiful new Scandinavian type Council Hall by the Mayor and Mayoress. The sun streamed through the windows on us as we all received a commemorative pen!

One Sunday we walked in the park round a frozen pond to the Museum, where there was a fine Edward Burra exhibition. We liked his later paintings best as they are not so meaty. Afterwards we visited the little Music Hall Museum next to our theatre where two gents were playing Vesta Tilley and Harry Lauder records on an old gramophone. My father would have liked that!

Switzerland, February 1977

We were soon on the road again to a job we didn't relish, but somehow the lure of appreciation, money and wonderful scenery won the day. It was only a month's slaving after all, to pay for an idyllic holiday thrown in afterwards.

More new stretches of autobahn made the journey easier this time and we drew into a layby just before we got to Dôle. A Mendelssohn violin concerto on the radio helped to drown traffic sound, and send us to sleep.

Next morning we bought Sunday papers in Joigny, a little place where they were skiing and tobogganing on fluorescent sleighs in the sun and snow. It looked very Disney.

The work was a pill to be swallowed; the first show was at half-past ten, and the second at half-past one in the morning; then it was off towards Evian to the deserted camp by the lake in beautiful Switzerland.

We spent a lovely week's holiday up high in the mountains at Anzère before returning home to prepare for a week in Bristol Hippodrome Theatre. John Redgrave had been asked to provide a week's entertainment for the over-70s twice a day. It was the same show as we were required to participate in at Eastbourne that summer. We had not worked for Redgrave before and were told one of the Dior Dancers had recommended us, though I believe they considered us to be dancers – as indeed we were once. Joe Church carried the show as an excellent comedian, and John

Boulter from the Black and White Minstrels had a very nice voice. It was a lovely audience after the boozed-up one we'd had to entertain recently, and we earned gratifying appreciation at a cocktail party held afterwards.

Eastbourne, Summer 1977

In those days summer seasons and pantomimes provided artistes with good long periods of work and this one at the small Hippodrome Theatre particularly so, as it lasted from May to October. It was John Redgrave's show and did very well. He later put a musical show on at the Devonshire Park, and special concerts every Sunday in our theatre. Ann Harriman, a pretty soprano whom we knew from pantomime, sang in one of these and stayed in our home at Stanford when doing the same at the Lees Cliff Pavilion in Folkestone.

It was a busy summer. Eastbourne is in reach of London, and we were inundated with visitors and receptions. We stayed at the Pevensey end of Eastbourne on an enormous grassy hedged-in park where Twoosy discovered she had rabbits, and even a fox, as neighbours. She must have had bad eyesight or possessed less intelligence than we thought, as a rabbit on our approach had scuttled out of its burrow almost under our feet; silly Twoosy stood at the mouth of the hole gazing up at the sky as if it had departed on wings! We were on our way to the beach which was almost next to our van. I would swim whenever the days were warm!

John Boulter, star of the Black and White Minstrels, once again headed our cast of *Holiday Spectacular* with Joe Church as comedian, Pat Stark the singer, and Cathy Downey a tasteful doll dancing to Glyn Evans's harmonica and a ballet of Jan Lynton's. We were rather surprised to read we were the Guest Stars with the Magic Carpet! All received beautiful bouquets from the Council and a party in the theatre after the show.

Jo Noble had brought her elderly Mother to live in Eastbourne after Ossie died. The arrival of many artistes in the town, many of whom she knew, was in some ways beneficial. We would often go along to have tea with them and enjoy the Muppets on their TV; we especially admired Kermit and Miss Piggy.

October 1977

We were the last summer show to close in Eastbourne that year and I believe we had done the best business, though the theatre only seated 600.

We had managed to see some of the other shows, however, with Ronnie Corbett appearing and Billy Dainty. The former we had only seen with the other Ronnie in their TV show which was very funny, though we never really fell for the Armchair solo. *Oliver*, the musical, came in at the Congress Theatre; we were very impressed by all the performers, especially Roy Hudd's wily Fagin. Bill Sykes was superbly horrid, and Mr Bumble the same rotund gentleman we had seen in London with Joan Turner now playing opposite him.

At one of those shows, we saw Sigurd Leeder for the last time before he died in Herisau, Switzerland where he taught after leaving London and Jooss had returned to Essen. I had known him longer than Jack, having been taught by him at Dartington Hall in the dance school where Jack was never a student. He seemed very tickled with our Act!

Our last days were very busy, as we had had to get rid of one car having had the Isetta, a new little Mini Clubman and the motor caravan in Eastbourne. This meant an extra drive to Stanford for the two of us to deposit one car before the final exodus! We had friends to the last show, beautiful bouquets again and a farewell reception with drinks and nice compliments.

There was a new leisure pool near us where I had my last swim, the sea being somewhat chilly by now. Jo Noble was sad to see all the artistes departing. It had quite made her summer, mingling in her world again. She had many theatre friends living in the town though, and was a member of the local golf club.

Copenhagen 1977

Soon we set off for Copenhagen again and I will quote from the letter I wrote to Jo when we arrived at the *pension* where the 'Chat Noir' boarded their artistes.

We landed up on the thirty first at the stage door hoping to unload. Our letter to the management requesting access had not reached the Stage Director who curtly informed us that we could have written to him, as he had signed our contract! This arrogant Arab-looking gentleman told us we should have written to him as he was the producer and director of the show and hoped our act wasn't too long as the whole thing only lasted one hour. Jack and I knew immediately it was going to be very tricky. This man had that aura of 'Importance'. We soon discovered he was a refugee from Beirut who had had to flee when the war broke out the previous year. He had owned the Jockey Club and several others, and had to leave his flat and possessions all behind. However, we think we now have his respect but not adequate lighting. We have had to go out and buy more UVs at great cost. All is settling down now, though alas, we were last in for a nice room at the *pension*. Ours is clean but smells of the last folks' cooking (or feet)!

Working conditions were difficult, as they always were on small stages; we got our apparatus caught up so easily in the curtains. There were three acts, a Spanish ballet, and no one to announce us except a dreary tape machine which had also to play our music.

We knew one of the acts – the Hovens – from another time; he was a very good mime and Dutch; his assistant was German and chatted a lot! Later we would all go swimming, taking a Sauna after. It is eleven years since we visited Denmark and its quaint Byg Museum, with pictures of the old town. We learned how the barbaric English had sent volleys of cannon balls from their ships in 1807 on to the city, causing great fires.

We found we were putting on weight as a result of eating the delicious Danish pastries with our coffee on the way back from the swimming pool. Round the table we would discuss the shortcomings of our employer who was obviously a rogue and using the takings of our establishment to build similar ones elsewhere, leaving our Arab gentleman in command. We were surprised that our agent should know him well enough to send her acts to such a shady character.

We didn't know whether other artistes did the same, but we made sure we demanded 1000 Kroner every now and then and bought some very nice Danish goodies, such as a Rosenthal vase, decorated by the artist Winblatt.

Winblatt's exhibition house was a dream; so much of it I could imagine Jack had designed. He had so many 'One thousand and One Nights' themes, and elephants in procession on his pictures, posters, cushions and covers.

We decided to visit the charming village of Dragor, beyond factory sites in waste lands outside the city and beyond the great new Expo buildings. It was enchanting with its little hut houses and its traffic-free narrow streets. George, our manager, suddenly appeared one day, looking pale and worried. The boss had apparently been imprisoned for illegally smuggling money out of the country. We thought it would be nice to get home and offered to terminate our contract and forego further salary. George, now the boss, refused to accept this suggestion and so we stayed, with payment, to the end. We were then able to see a smaller Company of the Bolshoi at the Tivoli. The diary reads: 'All pretty dreary stuff with a diminutive company doing all the old crap.' We left on 1 December, paid by George who, we'd learnt, had once been a Bluebell Boy, marrying a Danish girl and producing two children!

Dublin, Christmas 1977

The man in the petrol station had to drain our tank, having filled it with diesel by mistake, then holing it in the process. I'd only discovered the fact when I demanded the Co-op stamps advertised with petrol. 'Oh, you don't get stamps with diesel,' the cashier woman said. Horrified, I dashed out to the rescue. We'd missed the boat by the time they'd fitted a new tank but there was a mucky old freight carrier sailing that night with just space for us fortunately, but little comfort.

Jaded, we drew up outside the Gaiety where, in the morning, Jimmy Potter, the brother of Maureen, our leading lady, helped us unload.

Same dressing room as eight years before, even some of the same faces. Frank O'Donovan, writer and producer, Ursula Doyle director, Thelma at the piano, Betty the stage director and, happily, Sean the same electrician! It was such a relief to arrive on a large stage with a friendly professional staff who hopefully remembered the rather awkward cues. But the theatre, now owned by Eamonn Andrews, was somewhat shabby with its gilded boxes faded for a lack of paint – as was Dublin in general, compared with richer places.

We were a little nervous parked on a wire-enclosed lot behind The Eamonn Andrews Studios – and indeed someone tried to force our door one night, but they soon made off when we shone a bright torch at them through the window.

There was a very pleasant park between our site and the theatre which was a nice daily walk for Twoosy, and for us. We spent the two free days we had over Christmas on the Dalkey Hotel car park, which was a quay over the water. They regretted that they were closing for Christmas but offered us free baths as recompense! We woke up in the mornings with a view of the sun shining on the sea and at night the moon shone directly over the winking lighthouse.

It was good to be playing to full houses packed with children and Christmas audiences enjoying us, though we did have difficulties with a different drummer – young, and unused to providing the percussion effects we required. On one night, at the start of our Act where I stood as a Siva creature with six arms centre stage holding little lights in each hand, there was a blackout and an embarrassing pause. Jack, used to situations such as this, thought to slip off stage to the rescue, forgetting four of my arms went with him! The electrician beat him to it and there were my arms travelling back to me in a hurry, completely ruining our dignified opening! We hoped the audience thought it some kind of Christmas magic!

Another night, Sammy Snake's threads broke and he thudded heavily back into his basket completely blocking the other snakes' exits. I found

myself fluting endlessly until junior was able to hop out and then it wasn't his turn. In the end I just had to push the basket off and start the next action or sequence. At times like these one always hopes that the audience doesn't realise the embarrassment that is going on on stage or sorrow at losing an amusing turn of events.

Still in Dublin, re-reading letters we sent and received at that time, I realise what a happy season it was. The Irish have such a capacity for enjoyment and we bathed in good applause from packed theatres. I wrote to friends telling them of the temperate climate, as we'd only had a sprinkle of snow once, and how, when the sun shone on tropical plants, palm trees *etc*, one could imagine one was on a bit of the Mediterranean coast!

We spent several weekends out at Clogher Head, where our friends the Kuhns had a holiday cottage. What a lovely beach just beyond it! Walter Kuhn, a Swiss from the Ballets Jooss, had married an Irish dancer; they had made their home in Dublin when the Ballet closed down and they had discovered we were at the Gaiety.

I wrote to Maya Rovida, who had been in the Jooss company with us in earlier days, that the Gaiety backstage was exactly as it was in 1938, except for a gaudy coat of brownish paint added to the dressing room walls where now the taps squeaked and the roof leaked! But the theatre was still open, managing to support itself without a town subsidy.

Mr Kearns and wife invited us to their handsome house one day for lunch, as he knew us from the old days. He was to retire as manager very soon. We talked of the Ballets Jooss; as it happened, we had just had a letter from Ulla Soderbaum telling us that Kurt was recovering well after a motor accident and had more or less given over the responsibility of teaching other companies his work to his daughter with the aid of Laban's dance notation. Apparently Ulla, Noelle De Mosa and Hans Zullig had seen *Pavane*, *Ball in Old Vienna* and *Green Table* in Cologne and were not very satisfied by the reproduction. Insufficient knowledge of the Laban Script had blurred the artistic interpretation.

The Pantomime ran into the first week of March. We had the usual fine bouquets and farewell party. Maureen Potter gave us the most attractive copper plaque, a copy of the original, depicting the four children of Leer who were turned into swans by a jealous mother-in-law. When her spell was lifted, they were by then so old that they were baptised and buried at the same time.

We said farewell to St Stephen's Green, and the derelict lot that had been our garden for the last eight weeks, and waved goodbye to the last of Dublin Bay as our ship slipped away from The Emerald Isle.

Teheran 1978

In the early spring of 1978 we found ourselves with our 144 kilos of baggage on a plane again bound for Teheran. This must have been through our Paris agent and our employer proved to be slightly anglicised, as a result of an English university education. His Night Club still didn't come up to our standards back stage, though the auditorium was most smart.

The Iranian comedian who appeared last on the programme was in charge of stage management and the dressing room behind was full of ballet, other acts, and the feathered costumes of the former, occupying all the hooks on the walls!

We were all European artistes and of excellent standard, living above the club and meeting by day over our balconies or sunbathing on the roof. Our old friends from Paris, Sheila Hancock's sister and husband Roy Barbour, were having to do a smaller act as Roy's stilts would have taken him up through the roof.

Having managed to get ourselves adapted to these difficult situations in space both on and off stage, we proceeded to explore the neighbourhood. We paid 500 Reals apiece to be escorted round the city's sights and treasures. We visited the great Shayad monument that had not long been built, where we went to the top and looked over great expanses of dusty deserts towards the town and snowcapped mountains surrounding it. The Persians having their new year in April, our employer Jalal insisted we pack into cars and trucks and join the great customary exodus into the mountains, carrying pots of new grass to sacrifice to nature. After that, our contingent made camp in a peach orchard for a party and barbecue, roasting a whole sheep as the evening got decidedly chilly. It was not exactly our scene and, as it grew dark, Jack suggested we should break camp and started to pack up, which we could tell was unpopular.

Several incidents, pleasant and unpleasant, connected with our last

Iran visit remain with me to this day. The first was that Syria had seized part of the Golan Heights, closing that frontier and changing our flight path. Someone had desecrated Charlie Chaplin's grave and stolen his remains! The UN Forces were arriving to keep peace in the Lebanon. And lastly, when we travelled along 'Suicide Avenue' in a bus at speed, it braked suddenly at the stop and hurled me into the metal bar of a seat, which embedded itself between two ribs, causing two very painful last days.

The 'get-out' this time, though not the smuggling job as before, was tedious and expensive, taking nineteen hours by the time props and baggage came slowly round the carousel at Heathrow at a coffinlike speed. And one of our boxes did indeed resemble a coffin, being black and large enough to contain the Magic Carpet paraphernalia. On our way through 'Nothing to Declare' a Customs lady stopped our suspicious looking load. We were able to assure her of the innocent contents, completely forgetting the baby Persian Carpet nestling under our fake Magic one! It is so pretty now on the floor of our hall nineteen years later. We also have a picture of Persians playing polo with a ball made of some shell-like material; much later we realised that they were using human skulls instead of balls!

How good it was to get back to our green piece of Kent but spring had arrived and there was so much to do. Mr Thorpe was too old for much gardening but kept the place clean, tidy and safe always. The horse who used our field had robbed us of a few saplings we'd planted – they were all it could find to eat in the last snows, no doubt.

Jack, as usual, in spite of back troubles and I with a rib mending after the erratic bus in Iran, tended to take on projects beyond our years and strength and needed a rest before setting off for a summer season in Scarborough.

Scarborough Summer Season

Jack was thinking of taking a colour page in the summer edition of *The Stage* newspaper as we had a reasonable date. We were to have the first half of the run with Mike & Bernie Winters as tops, and the latter half of the season with Ken Dodd. John Redgrave was producing, and told us we wouldn't be able to finish the first half of the programme, as Doddy wanted to be there with his Diddy Men (Diddy Girls to be exact).

We left on 8 June, spending the night at my sister's in West Haddon, arriving in Scarborough by evening. We found Roger, Redgrave's manager, struggling with an unholy mess backstage of the Opera House,

making it quite impossible to unload our great carpet stand. However, we were able to infiltrate smaller props and objects into our dressing room so we could sleep in the van at the back of the theatre car park. It was good to stretch our legs and breathe the sea air along in the direction of the Spa.

Scarborough is a gracious Victorian spa-like town with its two bays and castle dominating the scene. We had previously performed in a Magic Show here down at the Futurist Theatre. The Opera House is a nice large theatre but though money has been spent on the auditorium, the staff backstage had to cope with extremely antiquated wiring and equipment. The cast gathered up in the bar for a press party – all except Johnny Moore the comedian who was still on his way from Las Vegas. The press fellows seemed interested in the drinks, rather than the cast!

Fortunately, Johnny arrived in time for the first show and succeeded in putting a fantastic audience into the right laughing mood. Were we glad, because we followed him. They loved our little robin and we went like a bomb. JR said he'd never seen the Act look so good.

Jack had made a beautiful new Carpet, larger than the last, but in the second performance things didn't go so well, as no sooner had I piped my rope up to a height suitable for clambering on to the carpet, the rope decided to flop hopelessly to the floor. I have no idea how I got on that carpet that time. Jack must have been able to lower the contraption. This was never possible in cabaret without tricky gymnastics and urgent whispered instructions from Jack.

We were definitely feeling our age, as we had worked so hard keeping Barnstormers trim. Jack's knee was very painful from the Act and his arm from gardening, and I was full of aches and pains!

It was not a very good summer weatherwise, but as it wasn't a suitable resort for seabathing easily, we didn't care. Twoosy found her surroundings quite delightful and the bad weather sent the holidaymakers into our show.

Don Robinson, the theatre owner, turned up in our dressing room with a bottle of fizzy wine to celebrate the fact that advance bookings were very good. We drank the lot between us. No wonder we woke up next day with dreadful headaches. So bad for our hardworking muscles and joints to consume all that acidity! As a result of Jack's unbendably painful knee, we had to leave the final lift out and both gyrate earthbound with elbows locked instead.

We cherished our weekends, and explored parts of Yorkshire previously unknown to us; we would book into a hotel in some beauty spot such as Ravenscourt for a bath, sea view and a meal.

In the week when Mike & Bernie Winters left, Robert Luff of the

Royal Hotel invited us all to a sit-down buffet, where we listened to speeches from Luff and Frank Comerford of *The Stage* newspaper. The place was packed but we only recognised Doddy and Danny la Rue from the past and of course Mike and Bernie Winters from our show.

So Ken Dodd joined us halfway through the season with his Diddy Men. He still overran his time in spite of everyone else galloping through their acts for him – so much so that at night he was in danger of running into the midnight hypnotist's show! Nevertheless, we still considered him to be the Clown of the Century.

Before the end of the season, Doddy asked us what we were doing at Christmas. He was to head the Liverpool pantomime where we would gladly have gone had we not by then signed for King's Theatre Glasgow with Jimmy Logan.

We heard also that our friend Danny la Rue was to be in *Aladdin* at the Palladium – and there were we banished to another *Aladdin* in Scotland. There was now a magic carpet written into every *Aladdin* script, and we heard that one of Disney's artists, who was English, had seen our carpet long before the cartoon film was in the cinemas.

Soon we were taking leave of our kindly wardrobe mistress whose husband knitted socks *etc,* and to whom we were to send Christmas cards for many years. Goodbye to Charlie James, the lady singer who also still writes, and of course Don Robinson who gave a tremendous party at his sumptuous abode above the cliffs. He asked us to return the following summer, which was very nice, although we never did.

We felt pretty old after packing up in Scarborough and sorting all the theatre equipment for two cabaret dates to follow in Switzerland and Belgium. Jack's knee was giving him trouble – not to mention his back – and he went off to have his heart murmur checked; he had had this since childhood after winning some horrific race.

However, we had one of those rather frightening Magic shows ahead of us first, at the Hastings Rock Pavilion. As usual, there turned out to be too much equipment for the space around the stage, setting all the magicians' nerves on edge, especially a German act who had a far too ambitious back drop to manoeuvre. Their levitated lady had to be swallowed into a spider's backdrop web and disappear. For this difficult feat, another curtain had to be let in front of her and, because of these difficult technical manipulations, the producer put them on first. This disappointed them extremely – and more so when, without enough time or rehearsal, the lady failed to fall into the spider's clutches.

I remember the fright of so many magicians trying to find safe spots to harbour their precious props and secrets round a concert type stage when not performing. This was always a problem with shows given by only magicians, where stage staff are not present to allot them nooks and crannies backstage or among theatre flats and scenery. We had learnt, especially in Europe, how much borrowing of props and ideas goes on in the profession. We met many suspicious artistes and many friendly ones. We did realise only too well that a whole magic act could be ruined by a chance movement to a prop.

After the show, we all agreed what a marvellous act the Polish magician Salvano's was. We had admired him in Spain in the Florida Park. We had also seen Ali Bongo, an English magician, for the first time; he looked like a rather large puppet Sultan, excellent for children. There was a very nice puppet act – the Silhouettes – but each number maybe a little too long.

King's Theatre Glasgow 1979–80

You could buy a ticket for as little as 15/- (75p) to see us in those days – from the gods, that is.

We'd left Barnstormers at the end of November, dropping off Thorpe and Christmas presents in Leicester with the two families. Feeling rather tired after the loading up, we slept the night on a motorway car park, arriving to unload the following evening. Fortunately we were met by the most obliging and helpful stagehands. The theatre had a large car park at the back where we could park permanently and obtain electricity through the stage door window – all very convenient for what threatened to be a harsh winter.

Jimmy Logan headed the cast with Peter Kelly as second top. Both of them invited the cast to very nice parties at their homes later on. At one of them we were shown Harry Lauder's piano and Midge's daughter Twoosy charmed the gathering by playing it as she had been taught on her miniature dog's toy at home.

We had the greatest difficulty getting set for the first run-through performance – to which, unfortunately, all the dignitaries of Glasgow had been invited. Jimmy Logan had a slosh scene, as they tend to have in pantos where there is a painting session or a wash day, as in *Aladdin*. I remembered Laurie Lupino Lane's magnificent fluorescent fake soap, all over his person in a previous pantomime we did. That time we were not expected to follow it in the programme; this time we were, and they took so long to strike that scene of foam that the stage manager, nervously impatient, drew the front cloth too soon, revealing Jack as a black ghost still setting up our heavy props! Fortunately, Jimmy's slosh was taken out after the first show! This necessitated a small addition to the script which

Jack obliged with: a suggestion to send a magic carpet to rescue the princess!

We were invited to lunch with the Lord Provost at the City Chambers – at least they respected artistes in Scotland! We were able to sit at a table with artistes from other Christmas shows, so did not have to be on our best behaviour. It was a fine formal feast however.

During the season we went to see Charles Rennie Mackintosh's architectural designs at the University museum. While he was staying in Chelsea with Margaret Morris and JD Ferguson, Mackintosh had designed a beautiful theatre, but they had never had any money to build it.

We spent a large part of our professional life in Scotland, especially when we were independent rather than with dance companies such as Jooss, *Annie Get Your Gun, Carissima, etc,* when we stayed maybe only one week. We visited this country many more times to fly our carpet over Edinburgh, or Glasgow, or Ayr – any time the subject had an Arabian flavour!

By now were doing two shows every day, and were almost living in the dressing room. As usual, we decorated its walls with the many bright cards we received at Christmas; we must have despatched over two hundred ourselves.

At Christmas Jimmy Logan, dressed as Santa Claus, distributed all the gifts we had given each other.

As the snow began to fall we trudged up University Avenue to celebrate the New Year with Jim Hastie and Robin Anderson. Twoosy loved it but had to travel home in the white bag.

After all the Scottish Hogmanay cups had been drunk, we got on with a pleasant pantomime which brought in large and enthusiastic audiences. What better way of spending the cold wet winter months? Jack had a birthday, saying he didn't feel well. When I asked him why, he just said 'Old' – indeed, sixty four is rather old to exert oneself in an Act like ours.

Michael Coveney of the *Financial Times* gave the show an excellent write-up for all our pains, saying he considered it better than the Palladium one, which almost made up for not being at the Palladium ourselves! We were told that the manager of Sunderland was in, and that he would like to book us in there next year – our fourth visit. However, Dick Condon had suggested we take part in the Norwich panto, which we thought was preferable.

Saturday 10 February was our last show. We packed far into the night as usual, and set off through sleet and snow. Having made our way through snowy Pennines, we called in at the Burkes near Kendal. They were contracted to stage manage a show touring South America soon, using our bungalow in transit. We arrived home in time to escape horrendous snowstorms, though our barn seemed to rock dangerously in the gales.

In April we were due to start a season at the Ruhl Casino in Nice, but on the day we were to leave the milkman's dray passed the door and milk was needed for the journey. I chased him down the lane, tripped flat on my face, and broke my wrist in an effort to save myself. No Nice! We had to telephone Paris to tell our agent we couldn't come; she was far from pleased and sounded unbelieving and annoyed. And so were we at the thought of losing a well-paid job with no work booked for the summer – we were to have earned FF1000 a night, less commission and tax.

By June, my wrist was sufficiently healed for us to take part in a week's variety show in the White Rock Pavilion, Hastings and then off to the Cliffs Pavilion, Southend – a nice theatre looking down on to a muddy estuary at low tide; we were able to park right beside it. When the tide came in, I would go down the slip in front of us and take a daily swim with Twoosy watching me from the bank. I never could entice Jack into water with me; he didn't like swimming. I suppose he considered it wasn't the most comfortable way to keep fit – and he seemed to have such a strong, healthy body almost to the end of his life regardless.

As children, sea bathing was always on our family agenda, and we made ourselves martyrs just to enjoy the exhilarating glow of its aftermath! This was on the east coast where the winds hurled high waves up on to Blakeney Point, the nursery to terns in the spring; Southend swimming was tame sport as the sea warmed up on its journey over a shallow muddy channel.

Up in the Cliffs Pavilion, business was quiet. True, the show was not studded by an all-star cast or fantastic top of the bill, and the locals had got out of the habit of having a Summer Season. Nevertheless, Jerry Stevens and Lennie Bennet were very good, the Harman Brothers we knew from a Bradford Pantomime, and there was also Alan Randall, playing the xylophone and banjo, very popular with an elderly audience. Alas, the coachtrippers to Southend climbed back into their coaches at the end of the day to go home instead of rounding off their outing with a visit to the theatre.

There was a very nice stage director attached to the Cliffs Pavilion; he and his equally charming wife came to lunch at Barnstormers one day bringing with them a bottle of Bacardi, their favourite drink. I had never heard of it before; we were not keen on it, but when thinking back to Southend, Bacardi comes to mind, because it stayed in the drinks' cupboard for so long, and its contents never seemed to become less!

When we were performing up North once, we had an invitation to visit Professor Eddy Dawes and his wife Amy at their house outside Hull. They had got to know us from the Magic Show we had done once at the Scala in London and must have decided we were worthy of being called magicians. We were very flattered to be included in this category as well as being modern dancers, though it was, we supposed, no more peculiar than a biochemist (which Eddy was in real life) involving himself with Magic. We enjoyed their company very much, and were invited to take part in one of the shows Eddy put on in Eastbourne. *The Book of Magic*, which Eddy wrote in 1979, received excellent notices and publicity and we were very gratified to find ourselves included in it.

At Dartington, besides mastering the Jooss–Leeder–Laban technique of the dance, we were also expected to notate the movements. This was I found, in its early stages, quite fascinating, but I was too impatient and left Dartington incapable of writing down a series of movements.

A half-American student friend of mine at that time, Ann Hutchinson, became extremely adept and later opened a Laban Notation bureau in New York. She married Ivor Guest, a dance historian, writing a book on Poirot as well as his Autobiography.

Ann returned to England and notated many ballets, including Jooss's famous *Green Table*; she now set up her office here; the last time we were in contact with her, she was scripting *L'Aprés-midi d'une Faune* and seemed continually to be off to performances in one country or another.

Nice, Autumn 1979

The South of France seemed more commercial than we remembered it eighteen years before. Tourists had left their mark and the bays around the beautiful blue sea were lined with those great white buildings looking like chests of drawers. The theatre was civilised with a helpful staff but there was no insulation between the numbers to allow for a change of scenery or awkward props. They like a fast show in holiday places.

Business was not good as the weather had turned wet and stormy. Workers on a high construction site at the airport, which is right on the seafront, were blown into the sea and drowned and we had to wade back to our camp.

We had some parties in, such as a group from a desalination plant who thoroughly enjoyed themselves and told another Act how much they enjoyed ours – which was rather tactless, we thought. Marly, the agent who had sent us to Morocco, came and told someone else that we were a clever Act! How we artistes love praise! But then, doesn't anyone?

Before we left the South, we revisited Antibes, Cannes and Monte Carlo, and the wonderful Musée des Marionettes above the town with its delightful clockwork dolls, one of which played a piano. That reminded us how glad our little piano-playing dog would be to welcome us back. We had slipped away while she was out walking with Mr Thorpe. She had known a departure was imminent and sat for hours outside the van to make sure she'd be a passenger!

Plymouth 1979

John Redgrave had recently bought the old Plymouth Palace. There was a small theatre on the Hoe, but the Palace was the only large one for visiting shows. How exciting to own a theatre and present your own productions!

John did not know that the Council showed no interest in the Palace because they were about to build a brand new theatre, which turned out to be one too many for a smallish town. As a result, he did not receive any financial support from the Council who had completely washed their hands of the old Palace; they obviously wanted it closed down. The *Western Morning News* of 27 November 1979 headlined an article 'Theatre in debt for rates bill'. It went on to say 'Impresario John Redgrave, whose efforts to revive theatre-going in Plymouth have met with mixed fortunes since he re-opened the Palace Theatre just over a year ago, could be in trouble with the bailiffs for not paying his rates. Last night he disclosed he had been issued with a summons. He owes about £4,000' – and so on. I don't know if it ever got paid.

We were engaged to take part in John's production of *Robinson Crusoe* starring Norman Wisdom. It was billed for a long season into March, and I don't remember a poor box office as a result of our efforts. It was a good pantomime – as were all those John produced.

We had the pop singer of the time Alvin Stardust, Donald Hewlett and Michael Knowles from the TV serial *It Ain't Half Hot Mum* and Dino Shafeek from *Mind Your Language*. We certainly always received the salary on our contract, but we were a little worried and aware that it came immediately out of the last box office takings of the week. As John had engaged a group of well known artistes of the day, he must have found it very difficult to pay their large salaries as well as his debt to the Council.

The panto ran as long as advertised and played to good houses throughout the season. It was a great pity that John Redgrave had to pay back Council debts out of the theatre box office takings because, apart from Norman Wisdom hogging the whole show after everyone else had cut their offerings, it must have been pronounced a fine pantomime, judging by the way the bus parties turned up. They obviously liked

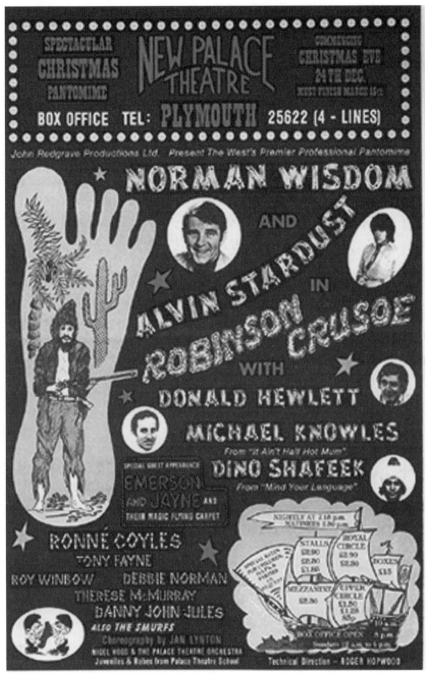

Norman very much – and so did we, apart from the way he overran the time allowed him! In Plymouth the curtain stayed up almost four hours.

The show ran until 15 March. Somehow John was able to keep the theatre open until the following year when we returned to fit once again into *Aladdin*.

One day we went to a matinee of *Jesus Christ Superstar* which was playing at the little Hoe Theatre. Oddly enough we had never seen it, in spite of its running at the Olympia Paris when we followed it with a Magic show. We could hear the strains of its music as we made up in the dressing room. I'm afraid we were rather disappointed with it but we were not really fans of the Lloyd Webber stuff. It is a very English taste though I am sure we would have enjoyed *Cats,* which is a permanent feature in London and was playing in so many of the European towns we visited.

After the last show on Saturday we would make off to Jack's tiny cottage beside the Tamar in Cargreen, if only to breathe the Cornish air and have a hot bath after our week's labours – two shows daily and wonderful audiences. Jack's ex-girlfriend from Margaret Morris days was staying there, having recently left the States and her husband behind with

Cargreen

a lady member of the college choir, where they had been teaching. We always said he had a roving eye when playing for the Ballets Jooss. Jack told Audrey she might buy the cottage cheaply as she had nowhere to go. This she did eventually but meanwhile we were able to enjoy weekends walking Twoosy along the river banks. Audrey's children joined the Foots Barn Theatre Company which toured Cornish village halls and commons. (Foot was from the famous Foot family.) To this day, Audrey gives dance classes in Plymouth; John Paul her son produces plays in Denmark, and Jenny her daughter works at the Royal Court. They attended our pantomime and so did a small granddaughter of the original Old Mother Riley.

And here is a strange coincidence. It so happened that when we lived in a small flat in Blackheath, we signed on with a doctor called Donald Towle. He told us that he was the son of Arthur Lucan (né Towle) and his wife Kitty McShane, who appeared on stage as 'Old Mother Riley and her daughter Kitty'. When Lucan died in 1954, Kitty took on another 'Old Mother Riley' – Roy Rowland.

Donald would tell us what a menace his mother was, often storming into the surgery threatening to ruin his practice. We later signed a contract for a show on the Isle of Man and found that Old Mother Riley was topping the bill and of course Kitty was playing his daughter as in days of yore. Luckily we were not staying in the same hotel!

The Towles moved down to St Austell with the practice but Donald unfortunately had a coronary very soon after. Later his wife Joan, reading that we were in Plymouth, asked for tickets for the pantomime and could Lucan's grandchild stand in the wings? This we were able to arrange. Clearly she'd inherited something of Grandpa.

We seemed always to be the last artistes to leave the theatre on the final night. We had so much heavy equipment in the way of lighting – props as well – to drag through the dock door and into the van. Last but one to leave was Norman himself, who said on passing the van: 'See you on the Isle of Wight'. So now we knew who one of the leading artistes was to be in our summer show; the others were Billy Dainty and Frankie Howerd.

Sandown Pavilion, Isle of Wight

We were unpacking for our Summer Season in a part of England we had never visited – how lucky we were to be able to see the Isle of Wight at last.

John Redgrave had not arrived, as he was still involved with his Eastbourne show so, after unloading into a nice modern dressing room with balcony facing the sea, we were able to take a rest. There was always so much to attend to at Barnstormers after a long absence, especially for the workaholic Jack, who would find something to do regardless. It was good to see him reading an Elizabeth Bowen novel instead.

It was a pleasant company, including Peter Goodwright, whose act we have always enjoyed. The tops of the bill were to change every month. Billy Dainty started us off with his funny and tasteful act which reminded us a little of Don Saunders. To follow him we got Ted Rogers – who arrived with a different wife from the one we had known when we were in a Fielding touring show starring George Formby.

After Ted, Frankie Howerd arrived, then Norman Wisdom and lastly Leslie Crowther. The audiences lapped it all up and they came in in good numbers as soon as the season got going. Frankie, strangely enough, didn't go down too well in his finishing spot; he was better when he appeared for less time in the first and second half. He turned out to be a very nice but rather shy person, who threw a super party at a hotel for the company before leaving.

When we arrived at the theatre one morning during the run we were met by glum faces on stage. It was apparent that something was very wrong. Our young stage manager had taken his girlfriend out after the previous night's show for a walk along the clifftop. We were told no more than that a rescue team had found his dead body on the beach below. The rumour was that he was into drink or drugs; we never were told the real cause, but he'd been a nice helpful fellow and we were all very sadly in shock for days.

We received quite a few friends from the mainland, including Arthur Lucan's granddaughter again, obviously stage struck. The weather was not always good for beach picnics but we were able to enjoy all the tourist attractions – those multicoloured sands down on Alum bay, and Osborne House, which Prince Albert had redesigned for Victoria with its wonderful grounds, and the children's little chalet. I have never forgotten the lace nightcap which Charles I is supposed to have worn the last night he spent in Carisbrooke Castle before he went to his execution – it looked so small and lonely lying there on exhibition.

By the time we had come to the end of the Sandown season John Redgrave told us that things were looking rosier for him, as a millionaire backer had arrived on the scene who would keep the Plymouth Palace open, paying off the debts and therefore ensuring that we would be getting together again for the next Christmas pantomime – that highly suitable subject *Aladdin*.

Meanwhile, another magic act called 'Zee' had arrived to take over from us as we were booked by our usual club in Geneva for October. He came up to our dressing room after our last show with a nice compliment and asked if he might buy some of our tricks. As the lucky man and his group were to do the Palladium that Christmas – which was also to be *Aladdin* with Danny La Rue – I doubt if we agreed! I'm sure there was a magic carpet in the plot.

Aladdin Plymouth 1980–81

Aladdin was always the most appropriate panto for our cod oriental act. In order to assure would-be patrons they would not be bored by any repeat of the previous year's entertainment, we were billed as Emerson & Jayne, with the words 'By popular demand' after our name. This looked very grand and impressed our friends and relations living in the neighbourhood immensely.

Audrey Cook, now owner of Jack's cottage, was teaching in California, so we were able to live in our old holiday home at Cargreen along the Tamar River, which was not far from Plymouth. Jack, with his usual zeal, wore himself out with two jobs – sprucing up the cottage's interior, and tidying up the overgrown garden.

John Redgrave, still our boss and producer, had been relieved of his commitments to the Plymouth Council, as the Palace Theatre had been bought by Stephen Kendall-Lane. He must have had faith in live light entertainment still being able to draw people from their television screens, for he had also bought the Phoenix Theatre in London, which show John was also to produce. Unfortunately the leading comic was not a strong enough draw; it received bad reviews and closed down, which dampened our hopes of ever appearing as a variety act in London again.

Our pantomime did good business as we had Dilys Watling as Aladdin; she had played opposite Danny La Rue the year before. She was a charming person whom we were to meet again in a Norwich pantomime. Also in the cast were Dailey & Wayne and Ken Wilson.

Instead of joining in the New Year festivities we watched television in the cottage, Jack being rather tired after his efforts in the garden and his one-man manipulation of the Act on stage (as usual, we found a good therapist for our aches and pains). We watched Jimmy Logan doing an impression of Harry Lauder, whose records my father had so often played. It could have been the man himself! We also saw a gruesome film, with Vanessa Redgrave giving an excellent performance as a Nazi camp occupant with shaven head. Michael Parkinson interviewed James Cagney showing snippets from his films. We never realised he was as good a dancer as he was an actor!

Paris again

We had little time between pantomime and home, as we were due on at the Milliardaire from the first of March. When we called in on Carmen on our way, she seemed certain that she could keep a second Emerson & Jayne in work on this side, so we realised that we had to spend all our spare time completing the costumes and props.

Until now, Carmen had sent us to exciting though not very comfortable engagements. We rather guessed that we were not one of her privileged acts, as we refused to become solely represented by her – and anyway we weren't French. In any case we had a family, dog, longer engagements on larger stages and upkeep of a self-made home on the

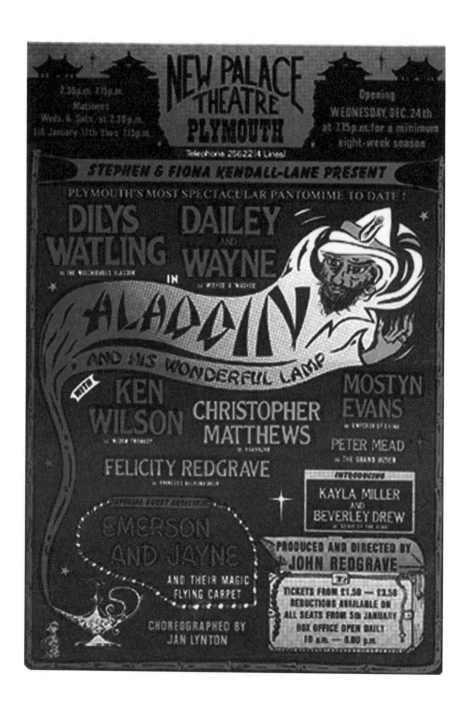

other side of the Channel. It would have been possible at one time to remain almost permanently at the Milliardaire; the management liked us as a replacement for the usual black-light act. This act, I venture to say, learnt a great deal from Jack's work, standing often at the back of the 'Saal' during a performance – but artistes, especially magicians, have always borrowed a great deal from one another!

We had worked very hard with the two who were to become Emerson & Jayne No 2 recently in the same shows. Felicity was a dancer and cousin of John Redgrave's; David Prout his electrician and her husband, a very knowledgable fellow in handling and working the props, admirably aided by Felicity. They went off on many difficult assignments in foreign lands, until Syria really got Felicity down with its Islamic restrictions. Unbeknown to us, she fell in love with a Yugoslavian stage hand when they replaced us once at the Hansa-Theater and we learnt later, when pantomiming in Bristol, that Felicity and David were to separate.

So, in March, back to the banks of the Seine and the camp – so far – almost to ourselves. Madame was always kind to foreign artistes, allowing us the hallowed pitches along the fence overlooking the river, though soon our privacy was to be invaded by *Holiday On Ice* caravans. They were however more civilised neighbours than most tourists.

Having squeezed ourselves and our props into the back quarters of the Milliardaire, greeted our friends, and battled with the first performance, things ran very smoothly in Paris with the help of an intelligent stage manager, formerly an artiste himself.

On our way home through the woods at night, we noticed many more prostitutes awaiting a steady slow-moving stream of cars than in earlier days. Frenchmen must have become even sexier in those past few years!

April in Paris; the audiences got better and we got an offer for Rome and Sun City in South Africa. Rome we were glad to turn down from past experience, and our Equity memberships forbade us to work in South Africa, unless blacks were admitted into the audience, which they were not at that time.

We visited a wonderful modern art gallery on the top of Pompidou's new Fauberg Colossus. What an impressive building! The gallery was reached by moving staircases and glass-walled passages, where we gazed at long-faced Modigliani paintings. The models with their close-set eyes looked so melancholy but perhaps, as the young painter had tuberculosis and was soon to die of it, his spirit manifested itself in their facial expressions!

Lowestoft Summer 1982

We opened at the Sparrow's Nest Theatre in Lowestoft on 4 July. The cast was excellent. John Redgrave may not have been a good financier but he had excellent taste in choosing his artistes, and it looked as though we should be in for a good run. It was a happy season with pleasant companions though to start with the weather was abysmal. All the better for business, no doubt, but the sea remained so cold and Twoosy, about to have her twelfth birthday, did not appreciate the wet either.

We were given a council welcome with drinks as usual, and a nice party at Don Maclean's place before he left and was replaced by Leslie Crowther. The latter took over the same house and also gave a party – some of us had to take cutlery, and I still have a fork with a fluorescent piece of sticky tape on it, which remains there in memory of Leslie, who died so young after his horrific car accident.

The stage door of the Sparrow's Nest theatre seemed almost on the beach in my memory, with a gracious park behind. It was a little way out of the town and a distance from the harbour.

We spent much of our time rehearsing Emerson & Jayne No 2 as Frau Grell, owner of the Hamburg Hansa, had arranged to come over and

satisfy herself that they were up to standard for her theatre. We needed them to take over from us at the end of November as we had to prepare for a panto in Nottingham. John Redgrave was away, and we had great difficulty gaining our resident director's permission for them to replace us for one night, but finally all was well. With much nervous excitement E&J2 took the stage in our spot and we sat in the audience. They battled through without any serious mishaps and Frau Grell agreed to accept them in our stead. They were then to go on to Rome after Hamburg.

Felicity looked very nice in Jack's newly-made costumes. I considered her hat to be much nicer than mine – I was quite jealous. She looked like a Botticelli painting.

It was strange how ultraviolet lighting gave a slightly flat effect and took the quality out of a strong movement. It was rather a discovery, but as the subject of our act was cartoon like, it didn't really matter unless one had been trained in Rudolph von Laban's dance method.

Theatre Royal, Nottingham, December 1982

Having seen Felicity and David successfully replace us, we left for Nottingham for what was to prove the longest pantomime run we'd ever experienced – it ran until Easter!

We could not believe our eyes when we saw our names in lights rolling along the façade of the theatre, together with the stars. Such a thing had never happened to us or the Carpet before, nor was likely to again – certainly not in moving lights! There was a great dock door at the side of the theatre, and we were able to drive our high Leyland motor caravan in and unload in comfort, for there was thick snow on the ground everywhere.

Barbara Windsor, who was to play Aladdin, strayed into this area by mistake. She regarded us rather scornfully and addressed us somewhat in the same way, but we forgave her later for the sake of her laugh and her performance, and she came up to our dressing room for a chat. We never had much contact with Keith Harris who shared stardom rather perilously with Barbara.

We enjoyed that long stay in Nottingham – it was not too far to visit family around Leicester and Nottingham friends of Jack's family. We also met Gordon & Bunny Jay for the first time; they were playing the funny police force, and we were in many shows with them later. Jack met up with an old pal from Margaret Morris days – Phyllis Calvert, who was performing at the Playhouse near us.

Our home was at the Yacht Club along the Trent, but we spent all our days in our large and beautifully warm dressing room with hot shower, whose walls soon exuded a Christmas atmosphere with the growing number of colourful cards.

Christmas Day was on a Friday that year: we had a lazy day – walking Twoosy by the river past companies of moorhens, reading the papers, and watching the Muppets on our portable TV. We were summoning up the energy for the many shows in front of us for, after the usual Boxing Day matinée full of overfed children, it would be two shows every day and three on Saturdays!

Keith Harris jokingly upbraded us for running away with the *Evening News* write up; before mentioning the cast, it wrote: 'What better tonic, deep in British wintertime, than a trip to old Peking (with a flying carpet excursion to Egypt on the side) in the superlative company of such a merry crowd as Keith Harris, Billy Dainty and Barbara Windsor?'

This was the most pleasant pantomime we ever took part in in our whole career, owing to the comfort, the length of run, a very talented and good-natured cast, and a sympathetic manager.

On her birthday, Phyllis Calvert came to tea in our dressing room and in the interval the Press summoned us to the dress circle to drink champagne at her request, for the sake of Jack's and her kindergarten days together.

The word always went around pretty quickly when there was an important management in front, and it seemed many came to Nottingham. We were told what an excellent performance Barbara gave and that she was to play next Christmas at the Cambridge Theatre. She told us how the manager Duncan Weldon had liked our Act and had said he'd like it at the Cambridge. Alas, this was not to happen. Having observed the Act with its necessary black drapes, use of back battens and decorative frontcloth, the management decided the hempen theatre ropes were not suitable for the strain! They had not thought this one out, for we had performed in many places without all our enhancing paraphernalia, as well as in hemp-rope theatres, to equal effect.

It would have been nice to record that our Act had graced the boards of a central London theatre – Adelphi Theatre Green Room Rags or Rats Revels, Chiswick, Wimbledon, Finsbury Park, Woolwich, Kilburn and the like hardly counted.

After we'd flown the Magic Carpet for the last time in 1994 at the Players Club, Jack wrote that the act had had its baptism there years before and it was right it should end its journey on that same stage in an *Aladdin* with the Charing Cross trains lumbering along over our heads.

Felicity and Dave meanwhile were not enjoying the clubs our French agent was sending them to. They were settling into a new house and would have preferred the English work we were doing, not having understood the nature of most work abroad. We were used to it, and had enjoyed appearing at doubtful venues for the sake of the opportunity of exploring new and exciting territory.

By now we were very loth to change with the opportunities fast disappearing for our type of act, and a house and dog to look after. Besides, we were nearing our retirement. Had we not signed for Cardiff pantomime finally and Babbacombe in the Summer as a result, we would have been very tempted with an offer for four months' work in Acapulco, fare and hotel paid plus £750 a week – not bad in those days. We'd always heard one should visit Mexico, and now the chance had come we were not free. Once again, we were enjoying Devon, this time in the little theatre at Babbacombe. With its tropical trees and bays, we preferred it to the South of France, but we did wish the water was as warm as the Mediterranean!

Through friends, we were renting a beautiful flat in Torwood Garden Road; we were able to put up visitors and several came, including an old flame of Jack's, Mildred Saunders, who now gave classes in Torquay and was an excellent swimmer. I would often join her at the Livermead Hotel swimming pool and later in the bay. I felt very proud of myself when overcoming the fear of diving at her encouragement.

Other visitors to the theatre were my brother-in-law Norman, anchored in Torquay harbour during a sailing trip, and a surprise visit from nephew Timothy, then at Exeter university, who has always been a faithful follower. Frank Green, a Margaret Morris friend of Jack's, came with his wife Kath to stay, as well as an aunt and cousin from Canada staying with them – a busy Summer Season.

The theatre was perched above the tiny harbour and looked out at the back down on to a winding steep lane. We kept our small collapsible sailing dingy down below and would sometimes sail all round the bay into Torquay, though we did have a tiny outboard motor for emergencies.

Top of our bill was a clever ventriloquist, Ray Allen, and the singer Kenneth McKellar who was to leave us before the end of the run for a concert tour of the USA and Canada. It was a pleasant cast, and there was little friction among us. We had old friends there from earlier times such as Glyn Evans and Cathy Downey who later married one of the musicians in the pit. We often wondered how Glyn carried on without a doll dancing to his harmonica.

Cardiff

On 12 December we left Kent in two vehicles. I was to put Fred Thorpe off for Leicester to spend Christmas with his sister, and Jack would carry straight through to Cardiff for pantomime at the New Theatre. Having

dropped Fred off at Victoria Station, I hastened off to join Jack who was already unloading at the dock door when I arrived.

Although we had been to this theatre at least twice in the past with the Jooss Company, we did not remember it at all. The billing was already plastered on the side of the theatre telling us we were to be with Ted Rogers once again, this time as the lead with his Dusty Bin. There was also the Welsh comedian Wyn Calvin who was new to us and Gordon & Bunny Jay whom we knew from Nottingham the previous year. We were sent in the van to live on a very good deserted sports club not far from the theatre with conveniences right outside our door.

As usual we had a comfortable dressing room where we spent most of the time for the next two months. There were three shows on Saturday (with extra pay for the third) and three days free over Christmas.

When I look back, I recall the various aches and pains we experienced in nearly every part of our bodies at different times, yet we would work over the pain and, for some magical reason, one pain always cleared up before another made itself felt in another part of one's anatomy. Jack had the stronger body and was less prone to arthritic and rheumatic troubles, but he had to start putting drops in his eyes for glaucoma, which one would think would have made it almost impossible for him to manipulate delicate objects on a blacked-out stage. Ultraviolet light, the effect of which made the act so successful, very probably ruined his eyes in the first place, but it didn't seem to prevent him finding the right string or object when needed, however! After all, we were in our sixties in the eighties! So these painful limbs after a few hours of gardening are not to be wondered at in the nineties.

We spent Sundays recovering from Saturday's three shows with the newspapers, but we did do some trips around, often on our bikes with Twoosy in a box on the back or running behind.

One night after the show we went over to a party with the Porthcawl panto cast and others, where we met Don Maclean again. He was performing in Swansea and was with Chilvers, the manager we knew from our appearance there in the '60s. We drank vermouth and ate delicious strawberry cake. No wonder we were stopped by the police on the long trip back. They said the car was swaying about, and I said we were uncertain of the way – and they did not breathalyse us.

Israel, Hong Kong and Macau
Our second trip to Israel
29 March was not much of a birthday as we spent most of it cramming the Cabaret Act into our small van to take to the airport. The engagement in

Israel was just for Passover, so we planned to leave our vehicle on a long-stay car park. We set off at the crack of dawn the next day. Even on the plane, the refreshments told that we were in the company of Israelis, and we realised we'd have to get to like the boring matzos bread during the Passover.

We made our way to a large park, its many exhibition buildings devoted to different pursuits. It was set in acres of sand to be trudged through. Even camels were trudging around for one to ride.

It was all very primitive, especially our performance space, where we found a small raised makeshift stage with no wing exits, or the black curtains which were essential for a black-light act. Somehow, they produced black plastic, and we gave four or five shows a day without losing ourselves or the props over the perilous edges of the stage. Our audiences, sitting on benches, on the whole seemed rather mystified with our efforts. It was not as though they had planned especially to see our show; they had paid an entrance fee to the whole Park and were just dropping in out of curiosity.

We shared the bill and the makeshift screened-off dressing room at the side of the stage with Martin Grainger and his excellent puppets. The sun shone on us as we roamed about between shows and refreshed ourselves from various stalls; luckily, after our toils were over, we were given very nice lodgings – our own little chalet by a hotel where we fed morning and evening.

At the end of our stay, as on our previous visit, we took a taxi to the Bethlehem Holy places. It seemed more exploited than in 1975; we went into the Church of the Nativity and down the grottos to the supposed spot of Jesus's birth, then back to Jerusalem and through the Jaffa Gate in the wall. In the quaint old Moslem street where it was necessary to bargain for everything, and where we had previously purchased the heavy old padlock we now have on our bedroom door at Barnstormers, we bought Jack sandals and a plate each for us and Fred Thorpe. Two of the boys from our theatre bought some kettle drums very cheaply.

We were carried over to Macau on a ferry and amazed and flattered to see our names spread across a great placard as we descended into the hold, advertising us at the Pedro Theatre, Macau. Strangely enough, I have no memory of any other act on the bill – perhaps it was augmented by local artistes; we never met any other Europeans. No matter, it was the highest salary we ever earned!

Circus Ross Hanson, Holland, June–July 1983

This was the second circus we took part in, but this time it was less impersonal, and not because Equity ordered that we should be one of the acts to participate in a foreign company's show, as when we joined the Moscow State Circus at Wembley.

Charlie Ross, one of our employers, was an artiste himself and he must have admired our act when we were performing in Germany at the Hansa. We know this because we later saw him performing material he had borrowed from our snake section. He was appearing from a basket like ours, dressed as an extremely acrobatic snake, performing the most amazing contortions in front of a decorative type of palm tree.

However, at the Circus Theatre Scheveningen that summer, he and the theatre owner Hanson did not perform, but dressed up in smart dinner jackets and directed in front and behind the scenes. This was lucky for us, as the acts followed in quick succession and there was no ballet or compère to entertain while the stage was cleared and reset, so everything had to function like quick clockwork. It was not an easy transition to our appearance for the stage staff, as they had to pull temporary drapes across half the arena and lay floor panels down over sand, as we set our many props. All the time this was happening an aerial act performed the most dangerous feats above!

As usual, the first few nights were terrifying but we began to enjoy ourselves later, as the orchestra got bolder and helped with appropriate effects. We liked the Dutch; we felt closer to them than to other Europeans, and we had many Dutch friends.

We had stayed with Aart and Marianne Verstegen of Ballet Jooss days last time we were in Amsterdam; naturally they came to the show, embarrassing us somewhat by sitting in the dressing room talking rather than watching the other acts. Aart had been director of the Nederlands State Ballet after the Ballet Jooss had closed down and had a right, one supposes, to be snobbish about circus!

We have always felt rather proud of being considered suitable for circus, but as circus is really for children, and children like magical flying carpets, why not? We enjoyed the experience, even the tiring plodding over sand twice a day in funny garb, and the procession to the pier and seafront in costume to entice the sunbaking public in!

Carmelita, a pretty girl with two beautiful horses, was parked beside us outside the theatre; also lions, poodles, monkeys and a troupe of Polish acrobats; there was also a comedy motor car. The staff were so attentive and friendly too, and even presented me with a china ballet shoe full of flowers.

Some Magic dates

We left Holland after squeezing our equipment between two lion cages and into the van, and made our way down to Baden-Baden where we were to do a two-night stand at the Kurhaus, an elegant building and surroundings, familiar to me from the early thirties when Mama, Joan and I sat drinking coffee on the Jugendheim–Dresden journey.

We were greeted by a rather unwelcoming stage manager, who definitely gave the impression that he considered a magic show in the concert hall quite inappropriate.

The first night was the usual fiasco with an insufficiently rehearsed staff. The audience, exclusively magicians, were able to see many things that should have been invisible and, in spite of their giving us a very good hand, Jack felt obliged to apologise at our curtain call. Thank goodness the second night's show, open to the public, went without mishap. Jack refused to attend the gala dinner for magicians on the first night so we rested instead and enjoyed the scenery around us.

The next day, the first of August, we did a show in Liebenzell, a delightful little spa in the mountains. The rest of the month we were to spend living beside lake Zurich, performing once nightly in the small Bernheim Theatre, in Europa Zauber which Werner Hornung and wife Fee put on every year. We took part in it twice. Strange that we became famous as magicians, closing the programme on his show, and taking part in so many magic festivals. This was quite accidental – we were just carrying on where dance mime turned into movement and mime, with props and puppet animals.

We visited a dancer colleague from Ballets Jooss days, Maya Rovida. Unfortunately she was in a sanatorium in Brugge after a knee operation and physically in a bad way. We also met Ulla Soderbaum, who was in Zurich at the time: she suddenly appeared at the stage door, almost falling over our odd-looking carpet paraphernalia. She regarded this strange object with some bewilderment, not connecting it with us ex-Joossites at all. Jo Noble, widow of Ossie the Clown Prince, turned up after sitting, she discovered, next to Frau Grell from the Hansa in front.

Autumn 1983

There was not much time to enjoy the garden at Barnstormers, or to enjoy our little dog, as we were contracted to the Hansa again for October and November. Soon we were off on that Harwich ferry to land at Hamburg. We enjoyed that date though, in spite of calling it 'The Factory' for its fourteen shows a week! The audience was always so appreciative, we lapped it up like nectar!

Not having received an attractive offer for pantomime at Christmas, we signed up with Peter Duncan whose father, Alan Gale, was putting on a short Christmas show at Brent Town Hall. Peter was well known from *Blue Peter* on BBC TV, but the children that watched that programme did not seem to live in and around Brent.

We were not very familiar with this part of London, and since our time with the Moscow State Circus at Wembley it had become populated with ethnic families unfamiliar with our Christmas shows and too impoverished to pay for tickets. Christmas Day was just another working day to the parents, being of a different religion. Moreover, the BBC would not allow Peter to advertise his *Blue Peter* show; the result was an almost empty house for both Christmas shows.

Our ultraviolet lighting was used to do a skeleton act, and Peter did a comedy horse and a lot of pastry slapping. Vic Templar did some very good clowning with his comedy bicycle and there was also a tiny tots ballet from Hot Gossip doing a routine to *Anitra's Dance* with a pierrot. They had our front cloth hung throughout the show to enliven the proceedings.

We arrived home from the short Brent stint on the first day of January, to greet Thorpe, dog, nephew and his girlfriend, the last two using our bungalow for a few days.

About this time we read of Margaret Morris's death in the *Dancing Times*. She was 88 but had been teaching in Glasgow until she was 81 and, as I have mentioned already, was the widow of the famous Scottish colourist painter John Duncan Ferguson – and of course Jack's first teacher. Later she moved down to be cared for by a niece in England, but how well I remember them both in their Scottish flat as she cooked a meal for us in the old-fashioned dark crevice of a fireplace, at the time when we were putting a group together, prior to the Ted Shawn season in Massachusetts, which was to be called the Celtic Ballet.

We were due in Paris again by the eighth of the month so, after a repack and a trim for Twoosy, we were off again, arriving that day in the Bois de Boulogne camp at 6am. We claimed our 'Place Comfort' by the river and set off to work. It was twenty-five years since we first worked there and three since the last time. Madame looked just as attractive as ever and kissed us fondly on both cheeks in the French fashion. She told us business had been slack and they were now only engaging three acts, as was the Crazy Horse nearby.

Margaret Morris and her husband JD Ferguson

We knew the other two from previous shows and the performance went well that first night. The magician Salvano praised the act and told us how famous we were in their circles!!! We were always astounded to hear such compliments and wished they would bring us more attractive work in our own country.

Actually it was the fault of our Equity Union that we had to refuse a prestigious English panto offer, when one arrived that year. All members were told not to accept offers owing to some strike of stagehands or musicians at the time. Most artistes in commercial shows such as panto were Variety Artist members in those days one supposes, and were not bound to such loyalties.

During the two months at the Milliardaire we were invited to drink champagne with the owner of the Elysée Palace in Montmartre, who put on year-long Operettas. We agreed to go and inspect the theatre and see his present show, as he wanted to engage us for the following year. Alas, having seen the production, we discovered that, although the stage was suitable, the side exits would not cope with our flight off – moreover, that we would be required to remain for the duration of the show – a whole year. This was unthinkable so we had to graciously decline the offer.

1984

Most of my friends and relations seemed to have acquired children now over twenty and were talking of retirement.

Jack was 69 and said he would retire at 70.

We were the past generation already!

However, Salvano the magician very politely told us that we looked ageless, even on the small stage, on account of our physique, movements and smiling eyes. He considered eyes could look old, even in young people and vice versa. But one finds it much harder to smile when one's old and has less to smile about.

In the meantime, we knew that if an attractive offer arrived from someone who wanted us and we felt able, we should accept. But we didn't turn somersaults any more.

In 1984 we were to spend more time at Barnstormers for, after Paris, we had only three dates in our diary. Bernard Cotton offered us a Summer Season in Ayr; a Scottish Season would have been very pleasant but he required four different numbers with change of programme. We had to wait till Christmas before reaching Scotland again, when we signed up for *Robinson Crusoe* in Edinburgh.

Carmen Bajot phoned offering a job in Dacca but somehow we were not attracted to the idea of lugging our 100 kilos of baggage to unknown tropical Africa.

The next trip we made was bad enough, as we had signed for Israel with another French agent, Bernhard Hilde. It was only for five days to entertain during Purim, a carnival time for children. The shows were to be in the Haifa Auditorium, Mount Carmel, which we knew from the earlier visit was large enough for the Act.

Having completed the two days and two shows there, we found that we were expected to pack and unpack our large black crates several times on unsuitable stages in other towns, getting up at 5am to load up and make the journey in taxis too small for the equipment. We even had to perform in a cinema where there had recently been a fire and no one had cleared the stage of black grime! Our beautiful glowing fluorescent snakes were hardly visible after their first slither.

In July, after a hazardous trip to appear on Chilean TV, we had a super hotel where we recovered in bed and were able to see ourselves on a TV set in the room! But as for getting there – no one had realised that we had to have American Visas even just to disembark at Miami airport to change planes. Believe it or not, in order to arrive in Chile for the filming we had to return to Holland and from there catch another airline's plane which would not call at Miami. We called at Rio instead.

The following day in Santiago we visited Ernst Uthoff and Lola Botka. We had left them in America after the tour of 1942, when they took over the Chilean National Ballet. They now had a son who directed the American Hartford Ballet in Connecticut.

We didn't have much time at home in November, as we were needed for rehearsals at the Edinburgh panto. Canterbury Marlowe would have been preferable so near home, but would have run for a much shorter time.

Jack still went on signing contracts; after Edinburgh, we were set for Paris, Geneva and Hamburg again. Luckily, we never felt our aches and pains while we were performing.

We set off for Scotland in two vehicles, as Jack was to put our friend Nigel Burke off in Kendal and I had to deliver Christmas presents to families in Chiselhurst and Leicestershire. We were neither of us feeling very fresh as, in a rash moment, we had foolishly bought a Victorian house on Hythe seafront, thinking it would be nice to spend our last years down there. Jack had spent much of the time when he should have been resting sprucing the place up to a standard suitable for letting in the meantime. We let the lower flat to the Burkes, home from their Las Vegas managerial work, and the rest of the house was let through a Hythe agency.

We had played the King's Theatre several times before with the Jooss Company, in musicals and with Glyndebourne. We asked for a large unused chorus room we knew was up at least six flights of stairs, as we had always too much clobber for the more prestigious dressing rooms down below which were rather small.

Up in this dressing room we made the acquaintance of The Old Man of the Sea, Roy Boucher, at the time married to the leading lady, Una Maclean. He too needed space as part of his job was dealing with the welfare of the cast, so he had the other side of the long row of mirrors dividing us for his office.

Johnny Beatty, a Scottish comedian, played the leading role. Although the theatre did excellent business, the *Guardian* gave the show a very bad notice, writing that money had been lavished on a load of rubbish. Admittedly, although the costumes and settings were most luxurious, it was not a good pantomime – *Crusoe* is not a good subject. Roy was furious and wrote an angry reply to the editor, pointing out that, the costs of production had already been recouped through box-office sales!

The Observer's criticism was not quite so rude and as Roy brought the paper into the room for us to read, he addressed us with a mocking and rather teasing voice. The article stated at one point 'the best thing in the show is the Magic Carpet'. This, though very flattering, was also very embarrassing and we knew it would make us most unpopular. When notices like this appear, artistes tend to assume one knows a reporter or drinks with the press in the theatre bar after the show. Nevertheless, before this tactless article appeared we had had a nice cod picture of Johnny Beatty on a Christmas card, dressed as a frightful Christmas tree fairy! Jack also received a card with a charming poem on the back:

> There once was a Jack who killed big giants
> and another who messed with Jill.
> There was a Jack who sat in the corner,
> another a house he built.
> But you're not the type to climb up beanstalks
> and there's no frost in your act.
> But still there is magic in all that you do.
> Merry Christmas Jack!

There was no signature to reveal which of Jack's girlfriends sent him that poem – probably a nurse from Addenbrooke's, someone in the cast, or an old Margaret Morris friend. It was one more to decorate cheerfully the walls of the large dressing room where we spent the long matinée hours, writing to friends.

Christmas and Hogmanay seemed to go on for ages in Scotland – thank heavens for the many Asian shops, where we could buy food. We were invited with others to see the New Year in at Una and Roy's house, where Una had gone to the trouble to cook us a vegetarian Haggis!

Back in Kent, according to Thorpe's letters, they were having a hard winter with snow and hard frost. Stanford was almost cut off. It was cold in Edinburgh but the snow had not yet arrived and fortunately the theatre was well heated.

During our run, the Glasgow Council's entertainment chief and the theatre manager came to the show. The former gentleman asked us if we remembered him from the last time we were in Glasgow. That was six years before, but luckily we had been warned the man was in, and might ask such a question. We heard on the grapevine that we had impressed the entertainment fellow who, supposing that we would automatically be in the company at their 'Kings', told us we could live on council property with the van.

It was always difficult associating with such a large group of people in such close proximity as one does on stage. The germs are rife and lodge in the slightest breathless throat. At home, one would be moaning in one's bed; in the theatre, one had to appear on stage however bad one felt. In such cases, we would leave the stage bathed in sweat, feeling a lot better and the fever lower.

1985

After loading up, we got away from the King's Theatre and set off down the snowy roads homeward, sleeping on the first car park, a layby before Berwick upon Tweed looking over the sea. The next morning late we carried on as far as West Haddon near Northampton where my sister Viv and husband live. We were given a nice 'eggy potato' lunch; she had always kept chickens, though she very often lost a few to the local foxes.

After hearing of the various festive days our relations had spent together, with criticisms of trying elderly Godparents *etc*, we proceeded South in thick fog.

We finally reached home somewhat battered, and were most dismayed to find that some pipes had burst in our absence – not only at Barnstormers but in the house we had bought for retirement in Hythe. There was still much work for Jack to do to the upper flat before we could let the place, so while I unpacked after the pantomime, and prepared for the next Carpet ride back to France, Jack slaved away at the house. I think he liked house arranging as much as performing; in fact he would spend leisure time on any arranging or inventing.

The year in front of us did not appear very promising. We had had an offer to take part in Jerry Cottle's Circus in the Congress, Eastbourne, but received no contract – presumably our salary was too high for him.

There was absolutely no reason to sign up for work, as we had plenty to do on three properties. Moreover, a builder had offered us £50,000 for the sale of the front of our field upon which to build two luxury dwellings. This we agreed to do; Jack pointed out that this was the equivalent of five years on stage, so why go off on some of the unprestigious dates we do? But we do! We like to receive acclaim, giving pleasure to other people at the same time. Why keep talent boxed up at home when proved worthy of exposure? But the barn was draughty in this cold winter, and our van was cosy, so we signed for Paris and Geneva again.

Geneva again

We had been to the Pussy Cat twice before, and hadn't really enjoyed it. We did however love the opportunity of exploring Switzerland's lovely scenery and breathing its air, while being paid for the treat. After all, our families were having to pay heavily for their exercise over there on their skiing holidays.

We had left the large motorhome in Paris as the Pussy Cat rented us a very comfortable flatlet almost on its doorstep; the stage was small, so we were able to pack our smallest equipment in to the Minivan.

Wandering along the passages beyond our flat one day, I noticed the nameplates on some of the doors – Lulu, Suzy *etc*. No wonder the lift seemed mostly to be carrying male passengers. Were they the hostesses from our club and were we living in a brothel? We never had an opportunity to revisit the Pussy Cat for the owner, we learnt, had many other properties and decided to sell the club. He no doubt became very rich from the bottles of champagne sold through the services of these ladies! (We were told later that they were not the same ones we met in the club.)

We returned to England in early May, greeted by Thorpe and Twoosy and a batch of letters awaiting reply. We learnt that we could have summer in Great Yarmouth once again in a show John Redgrave was to put on – he had taken over the whole pier complex and Winter Garden for the season. There was a drive in from the sea-front promenade, so we parked the van by the entrance to the theatre. Young Danny Redgrave proudly showed us around the demesne explaining all the nooks and crannies.

We were to do a short tour during the season to Felixstowe, Skegness and Canterbury, the latter being only twelve miles from Barnstormers. I do not recollect the show being a great success. The Yarmouth show played to quite good houses, at least at the beginning of the season, so we hoped Redgrave was not losing money. However, according to the *Eastern Daily Press*:

LOSS FOR TWO MAJOR ATTRACTIONS AT RESORT

Although the Wellington Pier's summer shows were successful,
other facilities made a severe loss, councillors were told this week.
Mr John Redgrave, Theatre Services Manager, has appealed to
Yarmouth Borough Council for more time to pay off £10,000 he

owes for rent and rates in respect of concessions he operated this summer.

John told us Rod Hull, or the Emu, was not feeling very well and that we might be closing down a few days early. We did, and on 4 September set off home again, calling in at Southwold where I took Jack to St Felix, my old school. It was during the summer holidays, but the Bursar took us all round the splendid new buildings – workshops for art, carpentry, computer mastery *etc*, and even a swimming pool WE never had the luxury of. It was strange finding one's way around the old haunts that still dwelt so strongly in the memory.

Jack was very impressed by the size of the place in its grounds, looking over the marshes towards Walberswick, where visiting parents would treat us to strawberries and cream at half term, and fathers got beaten in cricket matches by the girls!

We were due back at the Hansa by 30 September in order to allow another act to move on to its distant engagement. So little time at home to tidy up, before leaving Thorpe and Twoosy once again, the latter now an old lady but still enjoying her walks and smells.

It's an easy journey to Hamburg if you catch the Scandinavian Ferry at Harwich; you arrive at Hamburg docks after a cabin's sleep instead of a wearisome car trip. It's expensive, but worth it when you have to battle with a difficult first night. You need to offer a good performance, which seldom happens until an orchestra has come to grips with what you are doing on stage.

The Hansa had until recently the best audiences of any variety theatre in Europe and we enjoyed going there, in spite of having to do fourteen shows a week. It had a very caring management, and we were given a good dressing room and our usual parking spot on the area where the old Hansa stood. We realised that business had slackened a little when, at the first rehearsal, we found the orchestra (never a Philharmonic), had dwindled to a few geriatrics and a new drummer who hadn't a clue about following movement and giving appropriate accents. It took a week before things ran smoothly and yet the first night is so important to artistes, especially if they have a picture in colour on the front of a brochure telling tourists 'Where to go in Hamburg'!

Other acts on the same bill with us never seemed so defeated by the musical accompaniment as we were, though admittedly some of them only required background music with a drum roll here and there.

We discovered we had Kazbeck and Zari in the dressing room next door who had 'pipped us to the post' when we believed we had been recommended for a Victoria Palace show earlier. Jack Hylton was said to have appeared to be slightly annoyed when it was revealed that they were the very English Denis Williams and partner. We got to know Denis well in conversations in the Green Room and found him a thoroughly nice fellow. His lady was not always the same partner and kept more to herself – no wonder; their Act was very polished and spectacular, cruel and sadistic, as only a Whip Act could be! I certainly would not like to be the female, judging from the post mortems we could hear through the dressing room wall! Jack and Denis kept up a correspondence – we were a dying breed, just able to manage the dying variety dates that remained abroad.

Scotland again

We couldn't have found a pleasanter spot for a Christmas season. As promised, the Council allowed us to live in the courtyard of their offices at Kelvingrove Park, and provided electricity and water. A river flowed gently past our site. Twoosy loved her morning walks; she was sixteen but still lively like her Dad and Mum!

We had the same cast as that in Edinbugh and opened on 25 November to a fantastic audience. They came in coachloads, and gave us wonderful applause for the Act. The Scots seem so much more on the beam than the English, and more open and friendly on the streets.

Maybe I say this as they seemed to like us. *The Scotsman*: 'Veterans Emerson & Jayne produce beautiful and comical effects glowing in the dark. Their carpet is so magical it flies right over the orchestra.' *The Herald* wrote that we were the 'Highlight of the Evening'. We knew we would not be very popular with other artistes after this and, though we were happy deep down inside ourselves, we were rather embarrassed.

We all got sore throats and colds one after the other and Jack had a big struggle with the rake of this stage. He preferred never to get help with manoeuvring the carpet; we always hoped to find a modern flat-surfaced stage in theatres and clubs. Jack was feeling tired; we wondered if we were doing our last pantomime!

We saw Henry Fonda and Katharine Hepburn in *On Golden Pond* on our free day, sentimentally American but beautifully acted on a theme of the former's eightieth birthday. We also heard that Hepburn had recently developed Parkinson's disease.

How sheltered and happy we were though, still doing the things we were good at in various places, sheltered from all the bomb explosions and hatreds the world over. It seems the population is so large, that there isn't enough ground to go round! Just too many babies. That's one thing the Chinese have shown sense about.

On Sundays we would go out to Balloch Castle and down to walk beside Loch Lomond as we had done on previous visits to Glasgow. Now we discovered the Burrell Collection, recently housed magnificently in Pollock Park outside Glasgow. It held many wonderful works of art – far too many to digest on one visit. The most that the canny Scot William Burrell had paid for an item, we were told, was £14,500.

There was a comfortable restaurant at the Burrell in which to refresh oneself. We were invited to the usual slap-up lunch at the town chambers before the show opened, and we did one show on Christmas Day. It was soon time for Hogmanay and Jack bought me the usual Boots diary to start another year with.

Barnstormers 1986

We were back after our Glasgow pantomime; we were expected to call in on all our families on the way down from Scotland, but the weather was harsh and our big van had to be doctored twice by the AA before and during the journey. It had stood too long in beautiful cold surroundings and needed a service, so I was the one who dropped in at sisters and brothers in my Mini Clubman on the way down, while Jack hastened on to Kent.

We had no offers for the coming year apart from an invitation to Israel for the Passover again. At our age, we did not relish the idea of five shows a day in the heat, much as we had enjoyed the novelty of the previous engagement.

We were also invited to take part in the Frankfurt Magic Congress which would have only paid expenses for the few days, and involved a long journey. All true magicians would flock to these events but we were only magicians by accident really, and very honoured to be considered as such. However we accepted that in England light entertainment as we knew it had disappeared, so we resigned ourselves to settling down to a little home life.

The lower flat in our retirement house on the seafront at Hythe was let to our Burke friends, and their dancer children were occupying our bungalow at Barnstormers. They were working up a small dance group for an engagement in Rhodes, rehearsing in the hall of the Hythe Cricket Club while their mother made the costumes. All went well at Rhodes, and it was followed by engagements on the Islands of Cos and Patras, but disaster struck when they arrived at a very nice hotel in the Yemen, and strife broke out suddenly. Bombs were bursting all around them and they were advised to shelter in the British Embassy. They lay down in the hotel passages while the Embassy itself was bombed. As it happened, the Royal Yacht *Britannia* was in the vicinity and, leaving all possessions – including stage accoutrements – behind them, they waded out to the ship off the sandy beach. Their clothes being soaked, they spent the journey home in sailor suits borrowed from the crew of the *Britannia*.

Jack had put several thousand pounds into this venture and now it was back to the Cricket Club to start afresh, this time for engagements in Greece. Things would have turned out so differently for that family had the group been able to perform in the dwindling entertainment spots of this country. But light entertainment acts like this had vanished, even from television.

The snowdrops and daffodils came and went and the spring turned into summer. Jack started to catch up with the work needed at Barnstormers. We could at last accept invitations, entertain friends and, later in the year, spend a little time holidaying on our own in the mountains.

Andrew Burton, the portrait painter, came to stay, regaling us with his family news. We had known them since the fifties, now split up and the children grown. Andrew lived on his own, surrounded by his paintings. We have always liked them but his daughter pronounces them not daring enough. I suppose we are old fashioned, stuck back in the Impressionist period. Anyway, several of Andrew's paintings adorned our walls, and we enjoyed gazing at them.

We entertained Roy Boucher and went over to his cottage. He was looking forward to performing his 'Old Man of the Sea' again at Christmas in Sunderland, but then heard that they wanted Keith Harris to top the bill, and his Duck Orville refused to get stranded on Crusoe's Island, so they had to think of another subject. So no Old Man of the Sea for Roy; we heard later that he'd got the part of Smee in *Peter Pan*.

Two people asked about buying the cabaret version of our Act. They presumably did not know how few openings there were for it at that time – had there been an offer, I feel sure Jack would have been tempted to sign the contract.

Then we received two invitations: one to appear in a show called *Salome* in Germany the following year, the other for an English panto in Motherwell. At the thought of wintering in that town, Jack wrote quoting a salary which proved too high for their budget. It was only a five-week run anyway.

We therefore decided to sign for Christmas at the Hansa – not without sorrow, as we would be leaving our 17-year-old Twoosy behind again. She would have had us Christmassing in Motherwell had she had the choice.

And so, up to Harwich, bound for Hamburg again. There's something peculiar about those ships, or the passengers, for we often seemed to have

Barnstormers

contracted a bug a few days after making that journey – perhaps the stuffiness of those little cabins was responsible.

Feeling below par was never very helpful the first week, when you had the nervous strain of giving your all to make a good impression, knowing the reporters and the management were in front, looking to see if the Act was as worthy of gracing their boards as before. After all, we were by now quite ancient.

To make matters more difficult, one act followed another without announcement, so we had to have all our equipment gathered ready in the wings each side. Jack stood stage left and I stage right, ready to dash on and set as many props as we could carry, while the previous Act took its bow. Now, at the beginning of our Act, I am charming what I think are snakes out of a basket. But, just as the preceding artiste was delivering his last lines, I realised my snake-charming flute was still in the dressing room up a flight of stairs behind me. So up I rushed, and all would have been well had not a magician spilt some water from his props on the top step, causing me to slip. The audience must have heard the frightful clatter as I tobogganed down the flight; my flute was unharmed, but I was covered with scrapes and bruises! I do not know how I was able to climb on to my carpet that night; luckily the stage manager had sticky plasters for such a fiasco. In spite of this, we were asked to extend our contract another month and the papers gave us excellent notices!

Over the Christmas season, when all were in their seats, the lights were extinguished and the Hansa usherette ladies in their Victorian-style frilly aprons and caps would parade through the auditorium, carrying candelabras of lighted candles. This gave a wonderfully seasonal atmosphere to the show.

The Germans make 24 December their religious day, so we had no performances on that day, but we paid for it by having to appear three times the following day! In the New Year it was icy cold, with snow banks all round the Hof, very quiet, as few cars were braving the roads.

We feared very much for our water pipes *etc* back at home, where the weather was just as severe, and very worried when we were telephoned from Kent with the news that Mr Thorpe, now in his eighties, had collapsed with a heart attack. However, he had managed to drag himself next door where lived a doctor; until we returned, he and Twoosy spent the time squeezed into the little flat down in Hythe with the Burkes.

Of our Hansa-Theater performances, *Das Organ* – the journal of light entertainment industry in Germany – wrote:

October 1985
Emerson & Jayne are not magicians but they present a most magical 'Oriental Fantasy' in black light. This delightful piece in fluorescent colours does not fall into the usual category, in fact, to my knowledge it is currently unique.

December 1986
Emerson & Jayne surprise with an excellent Oriental Fantasy, a true Fata Morgana in ultraviolet light, full of rare happenings among which a flying carpet completely mystifies the public. The whole number radiates enchantment, it seems to border on magic and its composition and execution are first class.

January 1987
Emerson & Jayne were prolonged, their magic carpet too of course. Again this month they lead the audience through a world of magic and wonder, light and shadow. As far as I know, Emerson & Jayne are the only two performing this wonderful Oriental Fantasy, it must be the only one in the world. Idea and execution are worthy of unlimited praise.

September 1991
With their perfect illusion from a 1001 Nights fairytale, this wonderfully beautiful Fata Morgana pulls every onlooker to the edge of his/her seat. With Emerson & Jayne one can dream happily and put oneself in an unfortunately nonexistent wonderland. Incidentally I have not seen anything else like it, or better.

October 1991
From last month two truly top numbers were prolonged, Emerson &

Jayne with their flying carpet in a once only colour symphony between light and dark and, until now never surpassed. A truly international top number.

The management sent up Sec (German champagne) to the Green Room on 1 January, which we put on to cool so that we could celebrate later. Very kind of them, but we had learnt on previous visits that their brand, when compared with a French one, is very disappointing the first time one savours it . . . but to give everyone the French version would have proved too expensive for such a large cast.

It seemed we were still not to retire after this for we received a letter from Dick Condon asking us to keep free for a Norwich *Aladdin* the following Christmas, and it was likely that we would do a summer season for Don Robinson in Scarborough Opera House.

On 2 February we caught *The Prinz Hamlet* down at the Landes Brücken in St Pauli and did a last bit of shopping. We passed the Operettenhaus, where we had once done a week's magic and noticed *Cats* was due to do a season there. Strangely enough, we have seen only one of Lloyd Webber's shows – *Aspects of Love* – it was not one of his best, nor did it run as long as *Cats*.

I attained the great age of 71. Jack had turned 72 already, and still we were signing contracts, mostly to get away from the hard work our beautiful home entailed – rather shocking our families. But somehow we, especially Jack, made extra work for ourselves. We had no need for three homes, though other people inhabited them most of the time. Jack was as adept at house repairs and maintenance as he was at making stage shows, and when at home would also assist friends in moving their homes or fixing their curtain rails! So the only way for us to enjoy a rest was to take a holiday in the mountains or perform our Act! We always remarked when at home that our stage life was far less strenuous.

Scarborough 1987

So, in July, we set off for Scarborough Opera House to perform in the Holiday Laughter Show. As usual, we were able to live right behind the theatre. We found the town of Scarborough even less worthy of being called a Spa than last time we were there. It was more like Blackpool, the audiences non-receptive and scarce. Don Robinson, our nice theatre owner, must have lost heavily on the show. Later we heard he wanted to sell the Theatre.

One had to descend to beach and spa level to savour something of the past. We had pleasant picnics in gardens up on the South Cliffs by day.

During the run we were interviewed by the *Scarborough Evening*

News who, as usual, asked how old we were. I never wanted to disclose this, believing makeup, costume, black light, a broad grin and our distance from the audience made us look much younger than we were. On the contrary, Jack traded proudly on his two-and-seventy years and still treading the boards.

Nigel Burke had told us there was a second-hand American Chevrolet motor caravan for sale down on the coast. Ours having turned seventeen years old, we went to have a look at it and, having ascertained its engine was as roadworthy as its luxury living space appeared, we bought the monster! We didn't take it on our next assignment as it needed a little of Jack's handywork to make space for us and our paraphernalia. It was definitely larger than anything we'd had before – and had automatic gears as did most American cars now.

John Redgrave was producing the Scarborough show; *Aladdin* usually required a magic carpet in this country and we were presumably the only people who had one at that time. Not so now; after Jack supplied another artiste with diagrams and instructions, he went on to manufacture a far more sophisticated carpet to run in competition with us. But Jack was a generous soul and we were getting old.

By this time we had taught David and Felicity the Act and after the summer season was over, they went off to perform it successfully among other magicians in Boblinglen, Germany, where they were thrilled to meet Paul Daniels, also appearing at the convention. After this they planned to take the act to Spain where the mother had a dwelling near Benidorm Palace and where Felicity was to dance in the show.

There was much to catch up on, when we arrived back in Kent, what with an overgrown garden, the cabaret Act to sort out and pack up for its new performers, unpacking and cleaning our Scarborough equipment, and also the barn and bungalow to clean ready for holidaymakers. We had now to sell the old Leyland motorhome, and fit out the luxurious Chevrolet to meet our needs, as we planned to take a little holiday in this new acquisition.

We had over two months before packing up again for the Norwich *Aladdin,* so we departed in the last of the summer sun for France and Switzerland, planning to enjoy a fortnight's rest.

It was very scary adapting to the left-handed automatic geared Chevrolet, which was also much wider than anything we had driven before, but even I soon got used to it. As usual we visited our Elles friends of Jack's above Pouilly – Pierre who, as already mentioned, had trained with Jack at the Margaret Morris School in England and was in a bad way, having suffered a stroke. It was the last time we were to see him before he died.

We travelled to Monica Johnston's home for a reunion to celebrate the pianist Martin Penny's MBE, also meeting Bunty Slack and husband to complete our Dartington circle of the past.

The Theatre Royal Norwich revisited 1987

We parked our cream Chevrolet and the Mini Clubman beside what looked like a circus company's van on the side of the theatre's large car park conveniently near the stage door. Being also cream, the Mini looked rather cute and very smart, lined up beside our great van.

We discovered our neighbours to be part of an acrobatic act called The Amazing Dingbats – and my goodness didn't those fellows bat themselves about amazingly! They were extremely comical, with unbelievably destructive antics that they performed on the sort of apparatus one meets in a gymnasium. They were a merry lot; two of them also played policemen in the panto. We watched them from the wings most nights while collecting our props together.

Topping the bill was Wayne Sleep, a lithe, perky Slave of the Lamp. We had never before met such a busy dancing slave in *Aladdin*. He would arrive at the theatre in a smart chauffeur-driven car, at which we were most impressed. Dilys Watling played Aladdin and Wei Wei Wong was an admirable Princess, looking the part so nicely. Our friend Robert Marlowe produced the show; he came from the same Laban stable as we did.

It was a good pantomime and got good notices. Several of our friends came to the show, two from my old school, pronouncing it the best panto they had ever seen! We started off with a charity performance and then had two days free at Christmas, which we spent visiting old Norfolk childhood haunts. Jack was 73 in January, and I was 72 in March.

Though we both groaned with stiffness after three months' normal civilian life at home, we soon got the joints unlocked with repetition of the act twice daily. It was worth three or four days' pain to be on the road once more. I grieved, though, to see the wrinkles appearing on my face and tried to cover them with the fluorescent makeup, while Jack still looked amazingly young for his age, with no wrinkles, brown hair and an excellent muscular figure. I wrote a sentimental little dirge which went as follows:

> One looks in the mirror some comfort to seek. It never lies.
> But the lie grows in your eyes.
> The clear-eyed young regard your face as once you did your Aunt's.
> You, now an Aunt yourself, behind its frame,

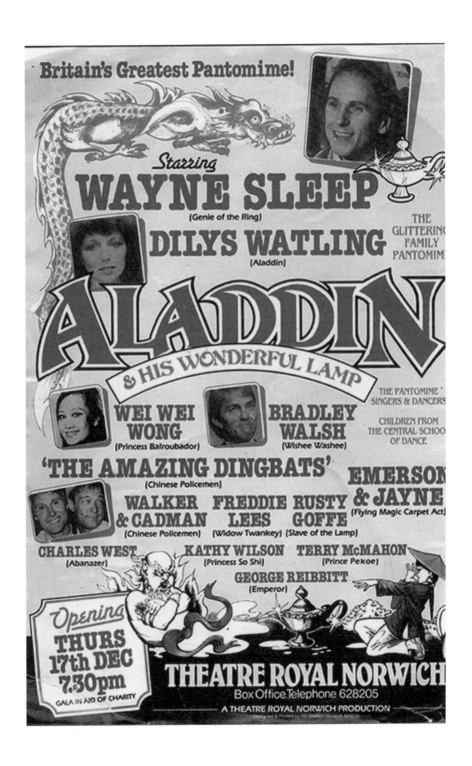

Feel just the same.
That face so cruelly drained of youthful grace.

Yes, in 1988, we were all getting old. The term the newspapers used was 'veteran' so and sos. We veterans Emerson & Jayne had a younger edition of ourselves now on the road, taking over the foreign dates but still only flying the small Carpet.

Jack told me for the first time he was really feeling old. He had had a fall and injured his knee while carrying Thorpe's heavy box of shopping in front of his chest, missing the pavement kerb. All our friends from the past were becoming veterans, retiring or dead! Don Saunders, who introduced us to the variety world in France, had died; so had Danny Ray who we performed with in Paris. Barbour and Billie were about to retire to a new home in Suffolk. Family and theatre friends, long retired, were obtaining new hips, new eye lenses, *etc*. Only a few of us Jooss dancers were still active in theatre life.

Ayr, summer 1988

Bernard Cotton was the manager of the Gaiety Theatre; we already knew him from two visits to the Alexander, Birmingham. He met us outside the Theatre, where we were to spend a very pleasant season, though we knew none of the cast, which was mostly of Scottish origin. Bernard directed us to an idyllic camping spot in Craigee Park, just outside the town. We paid £35 pounds a week and 80p to connect our home to electricity. Our windows looked out on to a border of yellow flowers and we were surrounded by trees.

The Gaiety is a charming little theatre with gold and purple cherubs peeping out all around. The stage, however, was extremely awkward for our large carpet manoeuvres. We were expected to present two different programmes, but we always managed to do the same act with only a few changes. We would start either with the Siva figure carrying candles, or with little creatures climbing on poles with umbrella tops. In the first show the cheeky little bird would settle on my flute and in the second show a frog would jump out of the basket. We would fly large and small Carpets in the two shows, in different directions. We also had different routines for our fluorescent streamers; in a show like this we usually incorporated the girls with smaller streamers which made an excellent finish to the first half.

While we were in Ayr, Jack prepared the prototype of our Christmas card. As with his advertisements for *The Stage*, he liked to air his flair for design and originality. This time he dressed up in his red finale costume, and one of our puppet snakes, twining around his body, held a cardboard painted Christmas pudding with cream and holly on top in its jaws. Jack sat in the corner of our dressing room, and I photo-graphed this apparition, which was duly sent off to our many friends and associates.

We had signed a contract for a panto at Bristol Hippodrome with Triumph productions. Les Dawson was to top the bill, and John Redgrave again was producing. We considered Les Dawson to be the best Dame after the late Norman Evans, who was Dame in the first panto I had ever taken part in at the Palladium. We were therefore rather shocked and disappointed to receive a letter from the agent to tell us Dawson had pneumonia and would not be doing the Bristol show. Gary Wilmot took his place, and we also had Frank Bruno the boxer, now turned actor!

As we never appeared with the rest of the cast on stage except at the finale, and we had a very nice large dressing room up three flights of stairs to ourselves, few of them left much impression. I do know that Gary was a good actor, and was certainly a kind fellow as he had once lifted us to a garage on the motorway when we broke down in the van. We also enjoyed his appearances on television.

The first days of the run were, as usual for us, most unpleasant. Norman Murray, who was not our agent, had his own act on the bill and resented the fact that we expected to take ten minutes of the show. He was adamant that we should shorten our act by cutting our finish with its extremely colourful flourish of streamers. Jack had a real battle of words but as we had our ten minutes written into the contract, we won the day.

Murray's artiste in the show was also a speciality act – a Duck – earning probably twice our salary, and having better billing.

We never had a sole agent in latter days, as we were working so much abroad and managements, knowing we were an asset to an *Aladdin* pantomime, would engage us regardless.

We always had musical difficulties when we met a new orchestra and this one was no exception. The percussion never once looked up at the stage to help with effects, and it was sheer chaos. We decided we would never do another pantomime,

The Bristol pantomime had a good run and when the orchestra got to know the act we got excellent accompaniment. It was always difficult to achieve co-operation with an orchestra when the music had been especially written to accompany the movement and effects of an act such as ours. We knew that the same *Aladdin* would be at the Dominion, London, the next year; it would have been nice to take part in it as our last panto, but agents need to make money from their artistes' commissions, so Duby Duck accompanied Frank Bruno and Michael Barrymore to that venue with the Roly Polys, but not Emerson & Jayne.

A French couple, who had been in The Omar Pasha Blacklight Company, flew to Glasgow when we were later performing there to see the Act and ask to buy. They were a nice couple and we felt dreadful in turning them down but somehow they did not look right; the lady was rather tall for the carpet ride and costuming, and we doubted if the man – who had not manipulated in the Omar Pasha Act but was a static performer having his head chopped off *etc* – could manage the technical work. We did not relish the thought of the Act being performed under our name by people who had no knowledge of the strength and dexterity needed to manipulate it, thereby lowering its standard. We knew by now that the manipulator had to be a cross between a magician and a trained athlete, to produce a copy of ourselves!

Felicity and David her husband had been long enough in the same shows with us to learn what was involved. We were very sorry therefore when, having consented to her new partner learning the act some time later, we heard that managements were able to take only what they needed from it for their pantomime productions. But then Jack was not there to insist that his work remained as intended.

There were no exciting travels to distant places this year, except a five-day assignment with Barney Colehan up at the Leeds City Varieties Theatre so before that, and after tidying up everything in Kent, we set off in the large Chevrolet on a little holiday; the last time we would enjoy its luxury. We had decided to change it for a smaller vehicle as Jack, owing to glaucoma, did not like driving at night. Moreover, I found it difficult to manipulate its width and length on smaller roads, though I did appreciate the unaccustomed automatic gear change and power steering. The Leeds show was in October, and included Charlie Williams; Joe Church, a comedian with whom we had often shared the bill; Lorna Dallas, an opera singer; John Bouchier, a ventriloquist; ourselves, the Pearce Dancers, and Johnny Dennis the Chairman. We had good audiences – 'Oldies' who enjoyed the show.

It was a pleasure to return to this famous little theatre, sadly neglected in its upkeep since the BBC left it, and now solely the responsibility of the Leeds City Council to keep it going.

Barney wrote a charming letter to us afterwards; it was not long before he died, and I wonder if the demise of the *Good Old Days* programme with which he had become identified was responsible. It had been strange meeting the subject of that *Have A Go* phrase of the past: 'Give 'im the money Barney!' And it's sad how quickly so many of the nice producers and managers we knew died after they were parted from the theatres they were associated with.

Now that we knew the long trips were over and we'd spent our last holiday in it, we sold our great Chevrolet motor home and had a smaller German van fitted out to Jack's design. Although we considered that retirement was upon us, his design still allowed us to transport the long Carpet contraption, though its end extended over our heads as we drove.

We travelled next in this way to the Eastbourne Congress Theatre; Professor Dawes had asked us to take part in a Magic show he was putting on there. It was supposed to represent the 1940s though we were hardly in costumes relating to that period!

We had to use a tape as there was no orchestra; we had often longed to do this on first nights so that the real orchestra could understand what we expected to hear from their instruments! Even so, calamity ensued. I had charmed my rope up high enough to climb on to the high carpet when it suddenly collapsed to the ground. The tape, of course, ignored this fatality and, as Jack struggled to lower the carpet under my posterior, it played the triumphant chord of achievement. Needless to say I rode off then in silence and astonishingly the audience clapped. Fortunately, all was well for the following show, as we were careful to protect the props more suitably in the wings beforehand.

The last days of Emerson & Jayne and their Magic Carpet

Autumn 1990

At the end of the month we left for Harwich and embarked on the old spruced up *Hamburg*, sailing late afternoon.

Little did we know that by then old Fred Thorpe had died in his little Age Concern flat at Lymne. He had been woken as usual in the morning but did not appear at the lunch table later. They had to force his door open when they received no response and found him dead in his chair. Poor old Fred's leg clot had travelled up to his heart, no doubt. His nephew phoned us the sad news to Hamburg. Of course we could not be at his funeral but my nephew was able to represent the family.

Poor old Fred. It was only four days earlier that he had walked by the sea with me and I had instructed him in the art of deep breathing. Hopefully I did not hasten his death as a result of the sea air!

Although the Redgraves had hoped Felicity would teach her new love our act, Jack was not keen for her to do so, and did not return the props, as he knew the new husband only as an electrician and stage hand at the Hansa. In any case, the Hansa declared that they would not want him on their stage as a performer.

During our last month at the Hansa, we performed the four thousand, four hundred and forty fourth show since the theatre was built. When the curtain came down, we remained on stage for photographs and all drank champagne to celebrate the event.

In Hamburg we missed our previous large motor home. There was a certain lack of space, and we had to tidy our bed away completely in order to create a civilised sitting room. It was impossible to spend a night in the vehicle when it was full of our Act material and we were in transit. Fortunately, at the Hansa, we had a spacious dressing room where we spent most of the day.

In due course, we accepted an offer to do a panto in Yarmouth – the idea of Christmas with less than the fourteen weekly shows we were expected to do at the Hansa was appealing. But, as it turned out, we would have been wiser to have stayed in Hamburg with the Hansa Christmas tree and candle Stimmung; the Wellington Pier show was no rave, with dwindling audiences braving the sea gales on their way to the ticket office.

From Jack's letter to a friend 18 January 1991

. . . I'm afraid I did not answer any letters during the Great Yarmouth experience, it was not without its difficulties for us to say the least, and much of my free time was spent in repairing things damaged in one performance in readiness for the next!

Now we are back at home, unpacked but not yet put away and I have set up the Amstrad in the motor caravan which now becomes my Office. The trouble is, now that my memory is so bad, after two months of not using it I forget its tricks and it keeps making a fool of me!

I am just about to become 76 and am more convinced than ever that it is time to retire; even Joy is beginning to feel the same, it is not that we can't do justice our act, we are OK in our black light but we do notice increasingly that when we get up in the morning we are old folk with aches in every joint and it takes until showtime to reach a condition which allows us to move normally and, perhaps, not look our ages!

Anyway, while we were in Hamburg (two shows a day, seven days a week!) we put an advert in the light entertainment journal to the effect that our 'Cabaret Act' is for sale and I have just been replying to some enquiries. As for the 'Theatre Act', which is what we've been doing in the Panto, we have already been asked to do next season's *Aladdin* in Edinburgh and I find it very hard to say 'no' but have suggested that we might have to teach the act to a young couple!

We have had long careers, Joy was dancing in Mary Wigman's group before Mr Hitler during the 1936 Olympic Games, and my first salaried engagement (£2-10s a week) was in *Peter Pan* in 1927!

Must finish now, keep well (and keep writing!). Love from us both, Yours, Jack

Jack spent much of the year refurbishing all three Acts, and we put an advertisement in *The Stage* that August with a view to selling all three versions.

Jack & Joy Skinner, long time operators of the flying carpet act EMERSON & JAYNE are finding 1991 more remarkable for the engagements that have not materialised than for those that have. Earlier this year they were offered a lengthy engagement at the Folies Bergères which fell through because of the scarcity of tourists in Paris during the Gulf War, the management closing the show for the duration, then later on, returning home from three weeks in Switzerland they found amongst their mail a telemessage from a Paris agent: 'CONTACT ME URGENT CAN BOOK YOU FOR WINTER ON BROADWAY'. This too could not materialise because they'd already signed for their 31st British Panto, a ten week 'Aladdin' at the King's Edinburgh!

E & J have been considering retirement for some years, in fact they took a full page of *The Stage* to make this known in August 1969! The act was launched, minus the flying carpet, at the Dorchester Hotel in

1953 when they had both retired from more legitimate endeavours in ballet companies and musicals. They now feel that, even in Black Light, it must be time to make way for younger folk and with this in mind they will be advertising their cabaret version FOR SALE while they are working it at the Hansa-Theater, Hamburg, in September.

We received many enquiries, and a children's entertainer called Jenny Wren travelled to Kent and carried our 'flying' version of the Act off – by this I mean the one that was required in distant climes where self propulsion was never sufficient!

Summer 1992 – Hornung's Magic Show

Before leaving for Switzerland, I was able to swim off Hythe beach. The sun was warm, but Oh! that cold shock of water creeping higher up one's body before one dares to duck! Once braved, how exhilarating it is, threshing around under the blue sky! And all is yours, far into the horizon. True, between Hythe and Sandgate, I sometimes had the whole panorama to myself.

It was so very hot when we arrived in Zurich that August that Jack even immersed himself in the Lake beside us of his own accord.

We always enjoyed those once-nightly Werner Hornung Magic shows. The trip from England had become somewhat easier by now as, once off the boat at Calais, we could drive straight on to the newly joined Autoroute 26 sweeping through France to Zurich.

Even the little theatre next door to the Opera House is on the lakeside in a pleasant park. We had already vetted its interior alterations for carpet riding, and before us Lloyd Webber's *Cats* had been stalking the boards.

Our camp was on the other side of the Lake and quite a bicycle ride away but we soon discovered we were able to take the boat across each evening and a bus home!

There was a charming Danish gentleman called Samson finishing the first half of the show who spent hours back stage concealing bunches of beautiful flowers about his person. He never looked suspiciously bulky, as he was slim to start with!

He then proceeded to wander about the stage, muttering crazy little doggerels, as if to himself, producing at the end of each one a gorgeous bouquet of flowers mysteriously from some part of his anatomy, until the whole stage was completely filled with colour. It must have been a well-thought-out production, because we terminated the show with a stage filled again with colour but this time from our brilliantly fluorescent streamers and flags.

We would stand in the wings prior to our entrance every night, having arranged the props in their usual spots for quick attainment, and watch the previous acts in wonderment. One of these was especially gruesome in execution. Two scantily-dressed Arab types appeared carrying a square glass box that a dog could have sat up in, and set it on a small table. The thinner fellow of the two started to show the audience how double jointed he was, by placing his right foot round his back to lock around his left ear. After other amazing contortions, he finally had the side of the glass box opened to step into. To our amazement, that man packed his whole body into this small box, by folding himself up into a tight enough package to fit it. His partner then picked the box up and carried him off in it!

Our last panto

We neither of us could have felt too decrepit when Dominic le Foe of the Players Theatre came on the telephone to ask if we would like to do the prologue for their next Christmas pantomime, for Jack got the urge again!

It was a nice idea to do our last panto in London in a theatre we knew, having already appeared there twice. Moreover, we could use the cabaret contraption, which required less energy, on account of the small stage.

We accepted, in spite of a request for the large Carpet to fly at Woking for another *Aladdin* which would have paid twice the amount the Players could afford. Britt Eckland was to star in that production and Jack agreed to loan them our large Carpet which we duly transported early in December. Of course, none of us realised that not everyone would find it easy to manipulate our version of 'Flight', taking into account the balance needed to perch in a cross-legged position on the Carpet, and the dexterity needed by the handler to steer the thing.

We had done this for years and were agile as ex-dancers are and, as we were rehearsing at the Players prior to opening, we spent only one morning at Woking rehearsing the stagehand who was to operate our contraption.

We were rather alarmed when Britt decided she must sit daintily sideways on the thing, as we knew it would so easily swoop her off. We could tell she felt this mode of rescue from Abanazer was not appropriate to a star, and that she resented any tuition from mere strangers.

The stagehand seemed to be able to cope with the weight and directions satisfactorily, but the exit through a back wing was always tricky when there was much scenery – it was essential to keep a clear runoff. We had to return to our own rehearsals at the Players, so could not spend more time at Woking. Obviously, they had not put enough effort into their own rehearsals for, soon after their *Aladdin* opened, we received an angry telephone call saying that the carpet contraption was lethal and

that the stagehand had allowed the counterweight to fall and had hurt his foot very badly. He had obviously had trouble backing off into the wings and its rider, we were told, had fallen off.

At this news, we could not help but smile a little wickedly. The flight must have been somewhat restricted compared with our usual one as the carpet – we discovered when we went to pick it up – was tightly nailed to its undercarriage so that it could not swivel and the whole thing had been made unmanœuvrable for any flight we would choose to make on stage.

We were able to watch our Players' pantomime, being on right at the beginning, for the reason that this *Aladdin* was set to start in a mining village instead of opening on to a gaily lit lanterned scene, full of scuttling little Chinese characters. So we were to be in the Prologue as befitted the title. We thought the show was excellent in its Victorian rendering of the subject, especially the fairy character of Ellen Macready. We were so pleased to find someone there as strong as Hattie Jacques was in the old days. And what a pleasure to have Geoffrey Braun still around playing the first night's accompaniments so much better than a first night orchestra usually does.

We always made an appearance in the finale and on the last night we had a big surprise when a lovely Chinese rug was let down on our heads from the flies. What a kind gift at the end of our Carpet journeys!

Jack wrote to our old friends and employers Dominic Le Foe and Geoffrey Braun when we reached home, thanking them for the happy Christmas season as follows:

> Dear Dominic and Geoffrey,
>
> Had it not been that Emerson & Jayne were a 'Dumb Act' they might have had something to say out loud to the audience and cast on Sunday about how much they had enjoyed their season with, if not actually in *Aladdin*, and how touched they were, as relative outsiders (their last spell at the Players had been in 1975) to receive the retirement presentation of that handsome Chinese carpet, the 'Good luck' card signed by the whole company, and the two Honorary Member cards!
>
> They are both agreed that the Players was, from their standpoint, the ideal place from which to depart, with pleasant memories, the profession which, not always so happily, has sustained them for more years than they care to remember.
>
> Here's hoping that under your directorship and aided by your hard-working crew, the Players will regain momentum and sail from strength to strength.
>
> Thanks again for everything . . .

We had met a young stagestruck boy called Roger many years before on our travels; he was then working as a stagehand in a theatre we were performing in and, as he had been most helpful, we tipped him as usual. Unknown to us this boy, now a grown man, had been in the audience for our swan song at the Players Club, and wrote to us afterwards with flattering compliments. Jack replied:

> . . . How extraordinarily nice of you to write to us after you'd seen the show at the Players. It's the kind of action that one sometimes thinks would be appropriate but I guess that most people (including me) tend to forget their inclination by the next day.
>
> This is just to let you know how grateful we are that you did write. After the last show, and the little party that followed it, we drove back to our home near Folkestone, Joy in the car and I in the motor caravan with the

props etc. We arrived home about 3am.

On waking late next morning, feeling rather bleak and hollow, I staggered downstairs to pick up the mail and there was your letter! Just what we needed to cheer us and to confirm what we have sometimes been conceited enough to believe, that our work may have had some value a bit above that of the average Spesh.

It was also nice to hear that your companion had thought we might be a young couple! I had my 79th birthday during the season.

You may like to have this photo to remind you of that Tip at the Alex in 1962, which I'm sure will NOT have been above average!

Good luck with your directing etc. We will be looking out for your name.

Thanks again and our joint good wishes.

It really had been a treat, performing 'Underneath the Arches' at the Players. We could not have wished for a more gratifying reception than that which our friends gave us at the last sold-out matinée.

I noticed that Jack was not well, as he preferred easily digested foods to anything solid I might cook. He would partake of a milk-like nourishment each evening on our arrival at the theatre; he easily tired these days too. The management had kindly given over its tiny dressing room to us – it was the size of a cardboard box, but big enough to house us, our costumes and breakable props. The rest of the cast were obliged to make up in one large dressing room.

It became a little embarrassing on those last days when our friends all chose to arrive at the same time and did not always know one another. It was wonderful nevertheless to see them again and be fed with their warming praise!

Each day we had had to deal with London traffic on the route from the excellent Crystal Palace camp, where we lived in a park with squirrels as our neighbours, to Charing Cross. In retrospect, we should have stayed in a hotel nearer to the theatre. However, we always travelled back to Kent in the small car at the weekend, leaving the motor caravan on the camp.

On the final night of the pantomime, as we flung our large coloured flags into the wings and bowed to the audience, we knew it was for the last time. The carpet engine was wearing out and so was the carpet rider. Both were truly 'Over The Hill with a Magic Carpet' . . . but they had been such happy flights of fantasy.